WORDS
THAT
FREE
YOU

WORDS THAT FREE YOU

What You Say
Is What You Become

Jacques Martel

FINDHORN PRESS

Findhorn Press
One Park Street
Rochester, Vermont 05767
www.findhornpress.com

Text stock is SFI certified

Findhorn Press is a division of Inner Traditions International

Originally published in French in 2011 by Les Éditions ATMA Internationales,
    Canada, under the title *Pouvoir des mots…qui me libèrent!*
First English edition published in 2017 by Les Éditions ATMA Internationales,
    Canada, under the title *The Power of the Words…that free me!*
Revised, updated English edition published in 2023 by Findhorn Press

Disclaimer
The information in this book is given in good faith and intended for information
only. Neither author nor publisher can be held liable by any person for any loss
or damage whatsoever which may arise from the use of this book or any of the
information therein.

Cataloging-in-Publication data for this title is available from the Library
of Congress

ISBN 978-1-64411-962-4 (print)
ISBN 978-1-64411-963-1 (ebook)

Printed and bound in the United States by Lake Book Manufacturing, LLC
The text stock is SFI certified. The Sustainable Forestry Initiative ® program
promotes sustainable forest management.

10 9 8 7 6 5 4 3 2 1

Edited by Jacqui Lewis
Illustrations by Josée Boucher
Text design and layout by Damian Keenan
This book was typeset in Adobe Garamond Pro, Calluna Sans and with
BD Supper used as a display typeface.

To send correspondence to the author of this book, mail a first-class letter to the
author c/o Inner Traditions • Bear & Company, One Park Street, Rochester,
VT 05767, USA, and we will forward the communication, or contact the author
directly at **https://atma.ca**.

Contents

Heart Symbol

This symbol, which you will find in the text, represents the energy associated with a mental image or an emotion related to a situation in which I am moving from my head toward my heart ♥, which then leads to a healing in love or to the reinforcement of a positive attitude.

Foreword
by Lucie Bernier

There is always a moment in our lives when we feel like making changes because we are dissatisfied with some of its aspects. This is often the case with our New Year's resolutions: I may decide to exercise, change my diet, take up a course of study, read books on personal development; and sometimes I even think that if I changed jobs or partners, I would be happier!

Although all these means are good for bringing about positive changes in my life, how about the words I use at each moment of my life? Is it possible that, whatever changes I may bring into my life, if I continue using negative **words** these changes may take more time to materialize? The answer is: Yes!

I have had the opportunity to experience this reality since I met Jacques Martel in 1988. From the very first personal development sessions that he led, Jacques taught me the importance of **choosing** to use positive **words**. I then discovered that each **word** we use carries an energy, a vibration that affects the person pronouncing it, namely myself, as much as the people who hear it. What a discovery! When I was first learning, the first stage for me was to concentrate on listening to myself speaking. I realized how much I, who considered myself as a "positive person," used negative **words** or expressions such as "*it's unbelievable, this is hell, it's dull, I just can't, it could be worse, this just can't be, it's not worth the effort,* etc.," to name but a few, and all this constantly, every day! Wow! What a leap of **awareness**!

Jacques thus showed me to gradually change the **words** I used for more positive ones. For instance, I learned that the more I focus my attention on the positive, the more I show something positive in my life. And that is what happened. An interesting fact is that, by doing so, my level of personal energy also increased! By using more *"This is great!"* instead of *"This is rotten,"* my life was becoming more marvellous! After several weeks of practice, I could no longer speak negatively because it no longer suited me. Even my body would react with a slight uneasiness to warn me that what I had just said was harmful for me.

That is when I really became **aware** of the **Power of Words** and that, if I carefully apply myself to change my words every day, I create a better world for myself and for others. Even surrounded by negative things, I can **free myself** from them because I keep focusing my attention on the positive!

In this book *Words That Free You,* that is what Jacques Martel teaches us. He shows us just how much our choice of the **words** we use is the basis for the whole change process. He helps us improve by making us become **aware** of the negative **words** we use, the harmful effects they have on us, the importance of becoming **aware** of them, and he shows us in simple terms how to make the appropriate changes, how to choose the right **words** to help us create our lives with more **freedom** and abundance.

~

Lucie Bernier is a therapist, Reiki master teacher, speaker, and workshop leader. The author of *The Little Stick Figures Technique for Emotional Self-Healing* (with Robert Lenghan), Lucie has also coauthored with Jacques Martel *The Encyclopedia of Ailments and Diseases.*

Introduction

S ince 1988, I have been leading personal growth workshops and often, in these workshops, I correct some of the participants' wording and explain the importance of doing so. I have been asked on several occasions: *"Has anything been published on this subject?"* I would answer: *"No, but I would see one day whether this was possible."*

The purpose of this book is to provide simple means for changing my language to gain more freedom, wisdom, and **love** in my life.

The **words** I use are the physical representation of my thoughts, the beginning of its materialization, and therefore of my actions. They shape the everyday life of the individual I am, of the being that I am.

And it is my responsibility, as everyone's, to clarify my thoughts, especially through the **words** I use. **The Power of Words** can bring me more healing and **freedom,**

> *For if Thought creates,*
> *Words manifest.*

"In the system of the Mystics, which has partially survived in the Indian yoga schools, the **Word** is a power, the **Word** creates. For all creation and expression, all things already exist in the secret dwelling of the Infinite and only needs to be manifested here in a visible form by an active **Consciousness**. Certain schools of Vedic thought even suppose that the worlds were created by the Goddess of the **Word** and that the sound was the first etheric vibration that preceded their formation. (. . .) It is said that men create gods within themselves by using the mantra,"[1] wrote Sri Aurobindo in *The Secret of the Veda.*

> *It is the most precious tool*
> *for entering the spiritual kingdom.*

And because the **words** I use create my reality, it is extremely important that they be exact and carefully arranged. Thus, the purpose of God's Thought is the creation of forms. **The highest form of architecture, in the physical worlds as well as in the spiritual worlds, manifests itself through its exactness in the construction of words and sentences.**

At any instant, at any moment, in any circumstance, I must pay great attention to the **words** I use and try to be in a state of **love** when I say them. In discussions about spirituality, **light** is often mentioned in relation to **Consciousness**, the spiritual worlds, the spiritual beings, etc. However, it is important to know that in relation to Creation:

> *Sound comes before the Light.*

---

1   Sri Aurobindo, *The Secret of the Veda.* Lotus Press (1995).

The Functioning
of My Brain

My brain is a super-powerful fifth-generation computer. We must remember that:

> **My conscious brain can hold up to 2,000 bits of information a second.**
>
> **My subconscious brain can hold up to 4,000,000,000 (4 billion) bits of information a second.**

This second sentence, regarding the subconscious, is extremely important because that is what my behaviour will depend on in my everyday life, my thought patterns, and so on.

In fact, at this point in time I am the reflection of my recent past, if I refer to my current life, or of my more distant past, if I refer to my previous lives.

> **It is vital to know that my brain cannot tell the difference between what is**
> - *Real*
> - *Imaginary*
> - *Virtual*
> - *Symbolic*

These are aspects that I must consider, especially in biological decoding as further explained in my book *The 5 Steps to Achieve Healing*.

I must be **aware** that when I say a **word**, both my conscious and my subconscious brains hear it, and the conscious and subconscious brains of the other person also hear it, hence the impact that this can represent.

Sometimes I speak to people about the importance of the **words** we choose. When I correct a person using the expression "*This is **hellishly** good!*" and advise them to not use this **word**, because of its negative impact, I often receive the following reply: "*But for me it's positive, I mean that it's extraordinary.*" I then explain to them that if I am in front of my computer, with a wide smile and full of nice intentions, and I write the **word** "*Hell*" to get the definition, it will surely not be positive, for this is the definition that my brain, my computer, registers each time I use the expression "*This is **hellishly** good!*"

I may not become **aware** of the results immediately. For example, if a drop of water gets into the attic, this will have no immediate consequences and none will appear for some time, but eventually an accumulation of water will build up in the attic and the ceiling may collapse. Then I will probably find that this situation is indeed "hellish" and wonder what I did to heaven for this to happen to me.

The Power of Intention

Words are important because of the effects they may have on me or on others, but there is an important factor I must take into account: it is the **attitude** or the **intention** I have in pronouncing these **words**. On several occasions, various people have told me about **words** or a sentence that were said to them and had affected them. I would then ask the person to tell me how they felt when I then said to them the same **words** or the same sentence. Often they would reply: *"Yes, but it's not the same coming from you."* They did not feel insulted; and yet I had used the same **words**, the same sentence, which, expressed by the other person, had made them experience an unpleasant feeling. I would then emphasize that it was not what was said, but rather the **intention** or the **attitude** with which it had been said that made the difference.

Words carry an energy, whether I want them to or not. The **word** itself, plus the intention I put into it, will determine the repercussions it will have on me or on others. If I hear the **word** "LOVE" said by an ordinary person, it is possible that I may feel something and that it may make this stronger feeling vibrate in me. However, if I hear the **word** "LOVE" said by a Master who has achieved Self-Attainment or God-Attainment, it is more possible that I will feel a greater wave of **love** flow over me, simply because this person is more **conscious** of that **word**, has integrated this aspect more completely into their life, and therefore manifests it more visibly. Thus, telling someone *"I love* *you*" with a sincere feeling will have more impact than saying it simply because I find it appropriate, without being truly and fully connected with the feeling I want to express.

Thus, telling someone they are a failure, an imbecile, and that they will never make anything worthy of their life may have different repercussions depending on whether I simply say it without making a scene or, on the contrary, say it under the influence of anger. In the first case, it's as though I were throwing dishes at them; whereas, in the second case, it's as though I were planting a dagger directly into their heart. Even if in this last case the act originates from an "impulse," I must be **aware** that the notion of 100 percent responsibility always applies. I may be "simply" distracted while driving my car and cause an accident that will kill one of my passengers or myself, but I will still be responsible.

The people around me know that I give out few compliments in general, including to those who collaborate with me, but that when I do so it is deeply felt on my part, so that the person receiving it will perceive it truly as a gift.

The Brain and
Homonyms

In 1988, I was at a friend's who lived in the country and whose house was surrounded by many birch trees. I was there with another friend, whom I shall call Pierre. Pierre is a very sensitive guy who easily feels the emotions of others and in which parts of the body they are located. He is a solidly connected man spiritually speaking and he does carpentry, for this helps him to remain more grounded. He feels very comfortable in this work.

Pierre tells me that, for several years, he was allergic to **birch trees** (*bouleau* in French, pronounced "*boo-low*"). I asked him at what age this began. He answered that it all began at the age of 18. I then asked him what had happened in his life at that age. He replied that he had entered a monastery. And, discussing it with him, I understood that he had had to let go of his work, his **job** ("**boulot**" in French, also pronounced "*boo-low*") as a carpenter, which he had so enjoyed, in order to enter the monastery.

This frustration or this loss had led him to develop this allergy to birch trees. In recent years, he had attended several personal growth workshops with another therapist and had healed the conflict at the origin of this allergy.

On French television, in a documentary about allergies, a researcher mentioned that of the allergies related to trees and shrubs, birch trees headed the list. Could it be that many French people who have this allergy are fed up with their jobs, with their "**boulot**"? However, research still goes on, doing blood analyses, seeking the factor that will cause the allergy to manifest itself…

In the South of France, a person whom I will call Paul who had attended several workshops with me told me one day of his allergies to **cypress** and **poplar trees**. He told me he was incapable of remaining in a queue for a movie ticket. That is when I understood that he had a conflict related to the fact of being "**so pressed**" (**cypress**) up close to people. He was also very uneasy in crowds, fearing to stand out as "**popular**" (**poplar**) among other people. I was thus able to identify the cause of the conflicts related to his allergies.

A friend, whom I shall call Louise, told me of her daughter who, when she had begun eating solid foods, was found to be allergic to **beets** (beetroot). I asked her what happened around her birth, and she told me that at the moment when her waters broke, she was still at home, and told her husband: "Luke, hurry up, let's **beat** it (**beet**), or we'll be too late getting to the hospital." The child had registered this stress and had developed this allergy to **beets**.

Someone who had tinnitus said that the sound resembled that of a **plane**. During a psychotherapy consultation, she was asked if she believed she was seen as "*attractive*" or "*plain*" (**plane**)… at which point a deep emotion revealed the conflict that she was experiencing with her family; that was the cause of her tinnitus.

The Power of Words
and Black Magic

I want to emphasize here a point that I find important and that we are not used to perceiving. Indeed:

> *Every time I point a negative thought or word at myself, I am performing Black Magic against myself.*

I have said that **words** carry a sort of energy within themselves. Thus, every time I depreciate myself, criticize myself, or feel guilty, these are all ways of turning negative energy against myself to destroy me. I may sometimes complain of not having been encouraged by my parents when I was young, or by the people around me or by my school friends, but what about my behavior toward myself right now? I now have the clear choice TO STOP DESTROYING MYSELF with negative thoughts or **words** and to nourish myself more with positive **words** filled with **light**.

> *Every time I point a negative thought or word at someone else, I am performing Black Magic against the other person AND against myself.*

When I send negative energy toward another person, I am sending them an energy of destruction. Now, there are two ways of seeing what happens to me. By the law of return, it will come back to me. Whenever I have these negative thoughts or **words**, I release this negative energy into my own energy field, also called my aura, which will come to affect me, whether I am **aware** of it or not. According to Yehuda Berg, a bestselling author in the field of spirituality:

> *The human voice expresses 99% of spiritual reality.*

My speech is a way of inducing spiritual energy to manifest itself in physical reality. In fact, EVERYTHING I say is related to my spiritual reality, whether I am **aware** of it or not.

> *Words are important, for they are the vehicle of this spiritual energy.*

It is obvious to me, on certain occasions, that I can "translate" who a person really is, just by listening to them speak. As the spiritual law states: "As above, so below," so the fact of listening to a person speak teaches me a lot about them. Whether the person is discussing a hockey or football match, politics or music, their comments inform me about who that person really is, and it cannot be otherwise. I can only speak about what is in my universe, and that universe is ME, the spiritual being who I am.

Several years ago, I became **aware** of a phenomenon that occurred inside of me whenever a person was speaking to me and I was listening to them speak and my attention was focused on them. In fact, sometimes certain **words** said by this person would resonate within me. I later became **aware** that this **word** or these **words** were connected to specific emotions of that person and could be related to the conflicts they were experiencing. I made several verifications, however, in order to find out if these sentences also resonated in me when they were pronounced by others. That was not the case, because those **words** did not resonate for the person who was repeating them to me, but only for the person with whom I had that reaction originally.

For several years, this capacity I had to feel certain **words** resonating within me proved very useful during the consultations and workshops I gave, which led me to follow and investigate this trail that I had and which logic, usually, would not have induced me to follow. And most of the time, it proved beneficial for identifying the conscious or unconscious conflict. When it produced no results, it was usually because the person remained closed off, refusing to investigate this trail, perhaps fearing what they might discover or the suffering that might surface. Thus, a person may tell me who they are or are not, but I will still know the real deal; and often I may give the impression that I believe the person so as not to enter into conflict with them, and let them continue their personal quest, even if I know that what they are telling me is false.

I may be listening to another person and/or myself, and I will be able to know, on many points, who this person is, whether the topics are spiritual, political, sports-oriented, social, etc. Indeed:

> *Under all circumstances*
> *I only speak to myself.*
> *The only person who exists*
> *in my universe is ME!*
> *All other persons*
> *are but the reflection*
> *of parts of myself.*

EXAMPLE

In the spring of 2010, I gave a series of lectures at the Salon MEDNAT, a health and well-being exhibition in Lausanne, Switzerland. At the end of one of my lectures a young man, whom I shall call André, came to see me to discuss his interest in the topics I had presented in my lecture as well as my book *The Encyclopedia of Ailments and Diseases.* At the very start of the conversation, in one of his sentences he used the **word** "**fallen,**" which resonated in me, but I didn't pay it too much attention.

In the following minutes, though, he used this **word** several times, so much so that I was surprised that he was using it so often; and each time this **word** resonated in me. Knowing that the **word** "**fallen**" is related to the conflict of multiple sclerosis,[2] I asked him whether someone in his family had this conflict, and he quickly replied "No." Later on, my insistence induced him to tell me that his cousin or his aunt, I don't recall exactly, had this disease. His initial "No" to my question must have been because he thought that it concerned only his brothers and sisters or his

---

2 See the text on "multiple sclerosis" in my book *The Encyclopedia of Ailments and Diseases*, Findhorn Press (2020).

father and mother. I explained to him that, for that **word** to reso-nate in me that much, the conflict of multiple sclerosis probably had to exist in him, but perhaps only at 10 or 20 percent and that he might never develop the disease. However, not knowing what stress his future life would bring him in relation to this conflict, which could increase that percentage, I suggested that he do the monosyllabic exercise with the text on multiple sclerosis in the book *The Encyclopedia of Ailments and Diseases* and to do an exercise from *The Little Stick Figures Technique for Emotional Self-Healing*[3] that involved placing on one side himself, André in good health and, on the other side, André with multiple sclerosis, and then cutting away the conscious or unconscious links of attachment that are related to this conflict and thereby diminish the percentage of stress.

The spiritual reality I mentioned above can be positive or nega-tive, depending on the **words** I use. Thus, there are the **words** of darkness, the negative **words**, and the **words** that bring **light** into this world, the positive **words**.

To become more **aware** of this reality, I made a list of the nega-tive **words** and a list of the **words** that carry the **light**, the positive **words**. By reading the first list, the one with negative **words**, I can amuse myself by experiencing how I feel when I read them. I can note the **words** from this list that I use and keep them on a separate sheet so that I can do the exercise of eliminating them from my vocabulary.

---

3   Lucie Bernier and Robert Lenghan, *The Little Stick Figures Technique for Emotional Self-Healing*. Findhorn Press (2022).

The Table of Negative and Positive Expressions

I can read these words with a hand over my heart ♥ to know how I feel when I say them. I do it with the words that tend to the negative and with those that tend to the positive. I pay special attention to the words or expressions that I use myself.

Negatively Slanted Sentences or Common Expressions That Manifest the Dark Side

It all depends	It's exhausting
It's a pain	It's his/her fault
It's dull (it's not interesting)	It's discouraging
It's fucked up (I can't understand it)	It's disgusting
It's rough (it's difficult)	It's difficult
It's absurd	It's hard
It's terrible	It's repulsive
It's no good	It's frightful
It's distressing	It's shitty
It's stupid	It's annoying

It's dreary	It's not easy
It's dreadful	It's not feasible
It's tiresome	It's not serious
It's idiotic	It's not fair
It's unbelievable	It's not wrong
This happens only to me	It's not bad
It's hell	It's not too bad
It's the story of my life	It's not possible
It's chance	It's not so bad
It's the end of the world	This is not your concern
It's total darkness	It's worse than . . .
It's life	It's lifeless (it's not interesting)
It's destiny	It's rare
It's deathly	It's revolting
It's foolish	It's stressful
It's panicking	It's silly
It's incredible	It's terrible
It's not my fault	This is dead (it's really not interesting)
It's none of my business	This always happens to me
It's not so great (It's not very good)	It's too expensive

It's not funny	It's too long
It's too heavy	**That just can't be**
It's too late	It's going to be hard
It's too . . .	It's going to hurt
It's killing me	**It's going badly**
It's a crime	**It's not worth the trouble...**
It's a real sin	Every time . . .
It's not rosy	For fear of . . .
It hit me	Don't get discouraged
It bothers me	Hitting a knot (it's blocking me)
It crushes me	**Don't worry**
It's beyond me	I'm afraid it's Yes
It's finishing me	I have no time to waste
It makes me sweat	**I don't have a darned cent**
It embarrasses me	**I'm afraid that . . .**
It grates on my nerves	I'm running all the time
It makes no sense	**I'm killing myself at work**
It doesn't bother me	I kill myself trying to tell you
It's not something you can say	I can't take it any longer
It's not something you can do	I'm not ready to . . .
It could be better	I'm down in the dumps

It could be worse	I'm sure not lucky
I'm disgusted	Don't forget to . . .
I'm tired	Don't feel persecuted
I just can't	Don't panic
I'm fed up	Poor little guy
The "I should have. . ."	To lose patience
The "Less . . ."	Don't waste your time
The "Nots . . . ."	Oh the misery
The "Maybes . . . The "Ifs . . ."	Life is cheap
The "Falling into . . ."	What a disaster
Don't miss that	How horrible
Lacking money	Just that!
Lacking time	It can't be helped
Darned money	Darned life
Less than	You disgust me
We're killing ourselves trying to . . .	You annoy me!
We're working like crazy	Go to hell . . .
We're working like nuts	There's no danger

Expressions to Discover and Use Frequently: A Vocabulary That Brings In the Light

It's cool	It's terrific
It's way out	It's considerable
It's open	It's correct
It's super	It's delicious
It's hospitable	It's supreme
It's admirable	It's divine
It's pleasant	It's gentle
It's artistic	It's dazzling
It's advantageous	It's resounding
It's nice	It's economical
Life is great	It's elegant
It's beneficial	It's elevated
It's helpful	It's enchanting
It's good	It's energizing
It's brilliant	It's enveloping
It's heavenly	It's spellbinding
It's warm	It's great
It's charming	It's aesthetically pleasing

It's sparkling	It's harmonious
It's astounding	It's fortunate
It's exalting	It's unique
It's excellent	It's impressive
It's exceptional	It's incomparable
It's exciting	It's unheard of
It's exquisite	It's interesting
It's extra	It's pretty
It's extraordinary	It's fair
It's fantastic	It's ecstasy
It's fabulous	It's a total pleasure
It's favourable	It's fun
It's flamboyant	It's the Med Club
It's flattering	It's paradise
It's formidable	It's seventh heaven
It's dazzling	It's tops
It's generous	It's luminous
It's kind	It's magical
It's gracious	It's magnificent
It's grand	It's majestic
It's grandiose	It's marvelous

It's cute	It's remarkable
It's monumental	It's resplendent
It's nourishing	It's rich
It's OK	It's gleaming
It's Olympian	It's salutary
It's appropriate	It's satisfactory
It's open	It's scintillating
It's perfect	It's seductive
It's special	It's sensational
It's perceptible	It's solemn
It's picturesque	It's sumptuous
It's pleasant	It's splendid
It's more	It's sublime
It's more than perfect	It's subtle
It's pre-eminent	It's super
It's preponderant	It's likeable
It's prodigious	It's just right
It's profitable	It's useful
It's really something	It's vibrant
It's radiant	It's alive
It's gorgeous	It works

It suits me	I love you
It pleases me	Nirvana
I prefer this	Stay calm
Give yourself a chance	You are brave
To marvel at	You are really extra
To get enthusiastic about	You're just super
To be ecstatic	You're doing that well
Trust me	You've got it
Stay confident	Appreciate
Keep your spirits up	Beatitude
I really have it made	Abundant
I've saved time	Admire
I'm eager	Attractiveness
I prefer	Ease
I take my time	Affluence
Yes, I can	Altruism
I'm in great shape	Amiability
I'm proud of you	To improve
I'm glad	Advantage
I am fully satisfied	A lot
I adore you	Beauty

Benefit	Decent
Well	Delicate
Well-being	Euphoria
Act of kindness	Exact
Seemly	Favour
Benevolence	Felicity
Good	Faithful
Goodness	Plentiful
Happiness	Fortune
Calm	Masses of . . .
Charm	Generosity
Compassion	To savour
Complacency	Grace
In keeping with	Grand
Consent	Harmony
Considerable	Honest
Contemplation	Humanity
Comfort	Indulgence
Proper	Infinite
Copious	Innumerable
Correct	Interest

Innumerable	Serenity
Interest	Service
Prettiness	Splendour
Magnanimity	Supreme
Magnificence	Very much
Many	Usefulness
Majesty	Vast
Leniency	Abundantly
Great Helpfulness	Pleasantly
Perfection	Amply
Pleasure	Considerably
Plus	Copiously
Several	Amazement
Profit	Enormously/Greatly
In abundance	Pretty much
Tranquillity	Largely
Delight	Marvelously
Harvest	Infinitely
Wealth	Perfectly
Salutary	Rapidly
Satisfaction	Rapture

Do you know **The Four Toltec Agreements**? Here they are:

> 1. *Make your speech impeccable.*
> 2. *Whatever happens, do not make it a personal issue.*
> 3. *Do not make assumptions.*
> 4. *Always do your best.*

In his book *The Four Agreements,*[4] Don Miguel Ruiz mentions this about the first agreement:

> "The first Toltec agreement: *Make your speech impeccable,* is the most important one and also the most difficult to fulfill. It is so important that by itself it will enable you to transcend your current life to reach that level that I call Paradise on Earth."

You may wonder here what the **word** "impeccable" means. Simply this: I must use the **words** that are **the most appropriately in agreement** with my inner being and represent the truth. **I must also always tell the truth whenever possible** or a part of the truth when it's possible to do so. Thus, if someone asks me what I will be doing this afternoon, I may tell them that I'll be shopping in town, even if I don't add that I will <u>also</u> be meeting a date.

However, the part I did tell them is TRUE. If I had said that I was meeting a colleague or something else, it would not have been true.

---

4 Ruiz, Don Miguel. *The Four Agreements: A Practical Guide to Personal Freedom; a Toltec Wisdom Book.* Amber-Allen Publishing (1997, 2012).

Thus, I can never be accused of lying. I do not have to say everything about my personal life or my business activities, but it is important that I maintain a definite integrity in what I say, so I then remain in the TRUTH.

The Power of Saying "I Know" Instead of "I Think" or "I Believe"

The following exercise is based on the fact that

> **As a SOUL,**
> **I can do everything,**
> **I am everywhere, and**
> **I know everything.**

It is by calling upon these qualities of the **SOUL** that I am that I will be able, in my speech, to use the **words "I KNOW."**

Thus, I can replace the **words "I think"** or **"I believe"** with the **words "I know."** Some have told me that this sounds pretentious. We need to better understand the context. I can say: "**I KNOW** how to cook," though I only know how to do eggs sunny-side-up with potatoes. But in fact "I do know" about 2 percent of how to cook. So I decide to take a cooking course and then I can say "**I KNOW** how to cook," but this time my rate has gone up to 50 percent, because now I have learned far more, even if I still have a lot to learn.

In the following example, I only need to read the written sentences while experiencing how I feel about each one of them. It is usually easy enough to feel the difference if I take the time to properly read each one.

- **I think** it is good to be concerned about the environment, for **I think** that we and the future generations will benefit from it. **I think** it can only be gratifying for everyone.

- **I believe** it is good to be concerned about the environment, for **I believe** that we and the future generations will benefit from it. **I believe** it can only be gratifying for everyone.

- **I know** it is good to be concerned about the environment, for **I know** that we and the future generations will benefit from it. **I know** it can only be gratifying for everyone.

I can also do the following exercise: when I listen to the radio or watch television, I can amuse myself by changing in my mind the text that I hear when someone speaks, whether it is a politician, a journalist, a person sharing their impressions about what is going on locally or on the planet, and this way too I can feel the difference.

On several occasions, when I have suggested to people that they use "**I know**" instead of "I think" or "I believe," they would tell me that they were corrected by their parents when they said that, because it seemed "pretentious" to say "**I know**." In the **light** of the new understanding that we have just read here, we clearly understand that "**I know**" doesn't mean that in our physical reality, "**I know**" 100 percent of everything I say I do, but in so doing I open myself to the likelihood that THIS will show up more quickly in my physical **Consciousness**, and I thus become more **aware** of my connection to the **Soul** that I am, who does KNOW EVERYTHING.

Another hesitation can come from the fact that when I say "**I know**," I am more connected to my responsibility toward myself and my higher Self. Indeed, when I say "I think" or "I believe," there is sometimes a great potential opportunity for consciously or unconsciously avoiding my responsibilities. In my opinion, this is the main obstacle to using the "**I know**," namely the responsibility it entails for me. However, there is a bounty from functioning in this way, and I am coming to it below.

> *Using "I KNOW" greatly helps me to be*
> *more focused on myself, on my higher Self,*
> *or on the SOUL that I am.*

It can also help me put all the chances on my side to get what I want. So, instead of saying: "I think I'm going to succeed," or "I believe I'm going to succeed," I say "**I know** I will succeed." I then connect more with the **SOUL** that I am and with the infinite power that is in me, so that what is good for me will come about.

Because "**I KNOW EVERYTHING**," I have nothing left to learn, but need only to **remember** what **I know** already. This will reveal itself far more quickly to my **Consciousness**, rather than me thinking that I must fetch something from outside of me to bring it inside. Now, **I know** I have everything inside of me and that I only need, by studying, to recall what **I already know**.

TESTIMONIALS

"I KNOW I can achieve Self-Realization and God-Realization"
. . . Oh my God, how pretentious that looks on my part!

And yet, after close to five years of saying that to myself,
the first part of that seems to me today to be quite feasible
and even, furthermore, well on its way to happening. Sure,
the second part still eludes me, as my intellect blocks off any
projection, but I KNOW that's how it will be, I KNOW that's
how it is!

Wow! I'm starting off hard! Why "I know" instead of "I
think" or "I believe"? Well first of all, to give myself a positive
instruction that suits a personal wish.

If I KNOW it, I am already focusing my attention on a
certainty that I need, in which I believe and from which I am
expecting a favourable outcome. In short, as someone I know
well would say: "I become that on which I focus my attention."

If I KNOW it, everything will come together at the right
moment, my life will begin to change and get better and better,
all sorts of ideas or connections related to the subject will come
to me. It will then be my job, of course, to apply what follows
from that!

And it is not necessary to believe it for it to come about!

I remember, about 20 years back, still unaware of any notion
of personal and spiritual growth and everything that goes
with that, I wanted to fulfill a childhood dream to go off to
Australia! For me, Australia, on the other side of the world, was
a country, a continent where I would certainly never be able to
go for want of the financial means and mainly because it was
unimaginable in my mind for me to ever go so far . . .

But my urge was stronger! I told myself that it would be truly
marvelous to believe that one day, my dream would become

a reality! I thought about it all the time, day, and night . . .
And then one day, there was a whole series of television
documentaries on the subject. I couldn't get over it. I could
already discover Australia in images and in depth! Of course,
that whetted my desire to travel. Shortly thereafter, I met some
people who told me about their fabulous travels in Australia . . .

Little by little, everything around me spoke to me about
Australia: a book, a film, an encounter . . . I must also add that I
was speaking to everyone about Australia . . . In no time, it was
as though all of Australia were coming to me! It was marvelous
and it excited my curiosity even more. I told myself that it was
a sign, that Australia was closer than I had thought and that
everything was possible! I knew, deep down, that I would soon
go to Australia!

I spent five weeks in Australia on our honeymoon (in 1991),
a trip that was offered as a wedding gift by our families and
friends! It was even more wonderful than I had imagined.

Since that day and with experience, I understood that by
building my life as I truly wish it, by opening up to myself, to
others, by having trust in myself and in others, I have better
chances of getting the information I need. I KNOW that I am
increasingly able to realize myself, to know myself better and
better, to be more who I am. And that delights me!

Of course, I don't say I KNOW everything 100 percent,
but even if it's only 10 or 20 percent, when I say I KNOW
something, I feel more confident, more self-assured, more
in harmony with what motivates me. It's as though I were
connected to another level of Consciousness and that fills me
with joy!

So yes, I affirm that I KNOW I can achieve Self-Realization
and the realization of God.

— *A.P.*

"I KNOW" is super powerful and sometimes I amuse myself, as you suggest in your lectures, when I watch or listen to the news, when I listen to the conversations of persons I know or mix with—storekeepers, neighbours, office colleagues—by changing, in my mind, the "I think" or "I believe" into "I KNOW." What power, what potency, what conviction! Myself, I try, as often as possible, to say "I KNOW" instead of "I think" or "I believe" and, as soon as I have made the conversion, suddenly my "I think" or "I believe" seem tepid and empty, as though I were talking to say nothing, without being engaged, but solely on a mental plane, and not at the level of the heart ♥, with its engagement in the responsibility of what I am saying. It's extraordinary, and it's by writing it now that I become aware of it. When I say "I KNOW," I have the impression of being engaged and aware of what I say.

— *C.L.*

The Power of Saying "Here" Instead of "There"

As we have seen above, as a **SOUL, I can do everything, I know everything, and I am everywhere.** It is this last aspect that I will rely on to use, as far as possible, the word "**HERE**" instead of "**THERE**." If there is an object to be moved that is located a few yards from me, I will therefore ask someone to bring me this object that is "**HERE**" to this other spot "**HERE**" where I am.

It is vital for me to understand that:

> *My reality is not my physical body,*
> *but rather the SOUL that I am.*

Several years ago in Quebec City, I led a workshop that was called *Inner Transformation*. During this workshop, which lasted several weeks, there were often guided meditations. When we reached the subject of the "**HERE**," there was a guided meditation that consisted in experiencing, outside of it, the sensations we felt when the workshop leader, during the meditation, offered the following suggestions:

I am HERE in Quebec,
I am HERE in Montreal,

I am HERE in Paris,
I am HERE in Moscow,
I am HERE in Tokyo,
I am HERE in Los Angeles,
Etc.

In fact, I do not move about, because **I AM EVERYWHERE**. It's important for my mind to register this concept, for it will be useful when I want to do what some call the **Soul travel**.[5] To simplify, I can say that instead of moving through space with my astral body,[6] with the **Soul travel** I am everywhere, and it is only the attention of the **Soul** that I am that moves about.

When I use the power of **words** and practice saying "**HERE**" instead of "**THERE**," I am merely training myself to experiment with this aspect of the Being that I am as a **Soul**. It's a useful exercise to open my **Consciousness** to this Reality that I am, this spiritual being that I am.

The "**HERE**" in question also relates to the notion of the "**HERE AND NOW**" that I mention regularly in the guided meditations. In fact:

> *The SOUL exists only*
> *in the eternity of the present moment.*

As the **Soul** is in the worlds beyond time and space, there is therefore no past or future for the **Soul**, but only the present.

---

5 © ECKANKAR: Here, Soul travel is different from astral travel.
6 Astral body: one of the energy bodies to which some people attribute the notion of astral travel in the worlds of matter, time, and space.

The Power of
Using "I"

H ere I take up an interesting point of language by using "**I**" instead of "you." What follows is directed to everyone, but more especially to people who work in helping relationships, to teachers, workshop leaders, speakers, writers, and people who lead guided meditations.

For several years now I have been using this approach of speaking as "**I**," especially in my lectures and personal development workshops, including in this book.

When I speak as "**I**," there is no psychological distance between the person speaking and the person listening. Also, the person listening doesn't need to translate in their mind what the speaker is telling them in order to appropriate the points mentioned as their own.

> *There is a powerful phenomenon*
> *that occurs when I use the "I":*
> *I am then "in resonance" with*
> *the public present.*

Resonance here means: an effect, an echo produced in the mind and the **heart** ♥.

Here is an explanation of the resonance phenomenon. If I place two pianos back to back and I hit the note LA on Piano #1 and then, after a few seconds, I mechanically stop the vibration of the string in Piano #1, I will find that the corresponding string in Piano #2 is vibrating at the same note as that in Piano #1. This is what is called the "resonance phenomenon."

Thus, when I deliver my lectures, I apply myself to use the "I" as often as possible when I explain something. And in case the participants' minds might interpret this as referring to myself, i.e., Jacques Martel, then during a lecture lasting an hour or an hour and a half, I may tell them: *When I say "I," I mean each one of us,* so that the interpretation is made quite clear.

Thus, in a sense, the persons attending the lecture "**hear themselves speaking**." Over the years, I developed this automatic practice of speaking from "I," especially during lectures, which occasionally leads me into situations such as: *"When I have abundant menstruation, it means . . ."* But in any case, people generally understand the process well enough. To carry it off more smoothly, I will often begin by saying: *"If I am a woman and I am told that I have breast cancer, then I know that it's because I am overstressed in relation to my child or my children, or what represents my children."*

In so doing, the contact with the public is far more intense. However, for a lecturer it demands a more disciplined use of language and many are not ready for that.

Thus, it may seem more natural for me to tell my audience: *"If you want this or that, you only need to do this or that,"* instead of saying: *"If I want this or that, I only need to do this or that."*

As a lecturer, when I use the "**I**," I feel more energy emanating from the participants in the room, and it's possible that some lecturers don't feel comfortable with this phenomenon. However, communication is greatly improved if I use the approach with the "**I**."

There are some people who achieve healing simply by reading the book *The Encyclopedia of Ailments and Diseases*, and the fact that it was written from an "**I**" standpoint may be one of the reasons that can account for that.

The Use of "I" in the Book
The Encyclopedia of Ailments and Diseases

When the manuscript was practically ready, I went in search of a publisher. I sent this manuscript to a person I believed was open-minded and who distributed other books in the field of spirituality. Faced with no response, I asked my associate at that time to communicate with the director to ask him what was up. The director answered that he and his colleagues did not feel comfortable with the manuscript because it was written from an "**I**"-perspective.[7] When he gave me these comments, I replied that I could make no concessions in this regard because it was part of a healing or Consciousness-raising process for the readers.

Writing from an "**I**"- perspective in this context involves, for instance, that instead of writing: "*If you are struggling with an infection, it's because you are experiencing anger . . . ,*" I will write: "*If I'm struggling with an infection, it's because I'm feeling anger . . .*" Thus, my brain doesn't have to "translate" to get from *"you" to "I,"* because it's as though it were addressed directly to the reader. Thus, my brain cannot say it didn't hear the metaphysical reason it has just read, which implies the notion of my responsibility regarding the infection. And this is how I operated sometimes when writing some of the dedications in the book *The Encyclopedia of Ailments and Diseases*.

---

7   I saw this director again in March 2002 and he admitted that he had made a mistake by refusing my manuscript, which as book quickly became a bestseller in Québec and Europe. He said his wife kept my book on her night table to consult regularly.

For instance, I would write something like this:

To Peter,
*I allow **love** to circulate more and more freely within me and all*
around me. I know that Life brings me everything I need. I put my
*trust in Life and will receive all the happiness I deserve. **Love** is*
the true healer.

Jacques Martel
Marseille, 26 October 2002

Some people have gained the false impression that I was addressing this message personally to myself because it was written from an "I" perspective and it bore my signature below it. This occurred with a therapist with whom I had attended a workshop in Quebec and to whom I had dedicated my book in this fashion. I only found out a year later that he had found me pretentious for having so articulated my dedication. I then got an opportunity to explain to him what it actually meant.

I have noted that about one person out of a hundred thinks that I wrote this text to myself, and there is a reason for that. It may be a protective mode where the person refuses what is written because sometimes, I connect with a person because I wrote something likely to affect them in a very personal way. I remember a therapist to whom I had written a dedication, in 1999, that evoked the prospect of "**accepting** ↓ ♥ tenderness in my life." I remember because I had previously never written such words to anyone else and I was surprised myself, as I did not know this person. Three years later, I better understood why I had written that.

TESTIMONIALS

I have noticed that using the "I" instead of the "YOU" acts differently on me depending on whether my eyes are open or closed.

For example, during guided meditations, which I listen to with my eyes closed, it's as though I'm giving myself a positive instruction to relax, an order with which I feel in perfect agreement.

I then truly have the impression of fully experiencing life in my physical body and I derive a great benefit from it. It's gentle, I have the impression of listening to myself. It's as though my inner voice were speaking to me, and I let myself be guided in total trust and safety for obvious well-being.

When I attend a lecture, my eyes are open and I have another approach. I feel that the lecturer is speaking of himself and of his experience, and I feel my eventual resistance to change evaporate. My mind relaxes, I open up more and I let go. I then hear better what is said, the information sinks directly to the level of the heart ♥ and I accept ↓♥ the conscious awareness that takes place in me.

What is always so surprising for me, and of course all the more wonderful, is that however I perceive things, whether my eyes are open or closed, the result is the same: I end up facing myself, with a wholly personal and positive understanding of my own experience. I see the situations to be resolved from a new angle, with the eyes of the heart ♥. I feel calm and thoughtful, serene and confident. The flashes of conscious awareness appear, because surely and undoubtedly this is the ideal solution for me, even if sometimes the solution turns out to suit me not at all or only halfway . . .

It is then up to me to decide whether or not this solution is the best one and consciously choose to go into action. And in any case, when I give myself enough strength and courage, while always asking to be spiritually guided and protected, and listening to my intuition, to my inner voice, and applying what I feel or perceive, knowing I am making the right choice, the light appears and healing takes place, at the physical or spiritual level.

I say THANKS.

Sometimes . . . often . . . I cry before such gratitude and blessing, even now, while writing these lines, because by the simple act of speaking, thinking, and writing about it, I'm experiencing it all over again in all my cells, and the whole healing process is happening again, as though by magic. I am amazed by all the possibilities and capacities we have within ourselves and that only ask to manifest themselves. And we only need to want it, be it at 1 percent . . .!

In conversation among friends, or during a consultation, using the "I" instead of the "You" seems to me just as appropriate: I have the impression of speaking with much gentleness and understanding. The other person then absorbs the information more deeply, opens up at the level of the heart ♥, which provides what they need to make it surface in their Consciousness.

— *A.P.*

The "I" is a powerful tool and I can confirm it, because I regularly listen to lectures and it adds an amazing force. Where the speech addresses itself directly to me, my brain does an immediate transfer with what is said and appropriates it easily, without the barrier of the "You." When I hear a sentence with the "I," I become, I absorb the information I receive from the person speaking, I AM this information, instead of HAVING this information. When I hear the "I," it is not general information, it involves Me. It's difficult to explain, it's easier to feel and, after so many years, it has become obvious for me.

The "I" enables me to feel unique, directly engaged in what is said. It better captures the attention of my brain, which feels immediately concerned and not lost in a sort of collective fog. When I hear the "I," I think Me, and the information comes in faster and deeper without the filter of the collective "You" targeted by the information. It's a little like the TV news, where the information that reaches us does not seem to concern us directly, and only engages us superficially, because it is addressed to all of us, as a whole. We feel less concerned individually, less engaged, and I am sure that if the presenter spoke as an "I," we would feel far more concerned.

— *C.L.*

The Power of Thinking and Speaking in Terms of "MORE"

It is a matter of paying attention to my vocabulary and replacing <u>all</u> the uses of "less" in a conversation with a "**more.**"

Example: Thus, instead of saying that something is <u>less</u> expensive and runs <u>less</u> fast, I will say that this thing is **more** economical and that it runs **more** slowly.

I can practically always replace a <u>less</u> with a **more.** And here is a list with **more** that shows I can use **more** to express what I have to say:

> **More** slow, **more** rapid;
> **More** expensive, **more** economical;
> **More** long-lasting, **more** short-lived;
> **More** easy, **more** difficult;
> **More** elevated, **more** squat;
> **More** robust, **more** feeble;
> **More** resistant, **more** fragile;
> **More**, etc.

Mentally, I will begin to think in terms of "**more**" and this will reflect itself in my subconscious.

When I think in terms of "less,"
I tend toward a limitation of Consciousness.
When I think in terms of "more,"
I move toward an expansion
of Consciousness.

The Table Converting the Negative to the Positive

CONVERTING THE NEGATIVE TO THE POSITIVE *

Positive formulations are as in the following example:

"During the 25 years that we lived together, we never lacked for anything" becomes: "During the 25 years that we lived together, we always had everything we needed." The idea is the same, but the terms used are more positive.

NEGATIVE Expression	Comments	POSITIVE Expression
I am **there**	Refer to the Here and Now.	Becomes: "I am **here**"
All the: "There's a **lack** of . . ."	The focus is on the lack	Becomes: "I **need** . . ."
I'm having **trouble** with . . . It's **difficult** . . .	The focus here is on the problem / difficulty, implying lots of heaviness in what I experience.	This **demands efforts to** . . . It **demands efforts** . . .
The **problem** is that . . .		The situation is that . . .
You **never** take care . . .	**Always** and **Never** refer to eternity; when I don't leave them an opening for things to change, I freeze them for LIFE. I should be more flexible.	You **very rarely** take care . . .
It's **always** the same thing . . .		It's **very often** the same thing . . . (It's like that now; but tomorrow it could change)
You **always** do like that		You **very often** do like that

* The information in this table was originally given to me by a person who attended my workshops a few years ago. As I do not recall his name I am unable to credit him appropriately but want to acknowledge this here. I have made some slight modifications to the information in this book.

NEGATIVE Expression	Comments	POSITIVE Expression
Here is some good news all the same (or even so)	"Here is" refers also to the Here and Now, the "nevertheless"; it virtually connects me to all negative ideas or events.	Here is some good news.
It went down well	Going down evokes the notion of falling, of hurting myself, and so in my life, I program some situations that will hurt me. The word "fall" also evokes the conflict causing Multiple Sclerosis.	It's turned out well
I'm going to die laughing.	Thus refers to death and to the programming that goes with it.	It's very funny
It's crazy, it's delirious!	I'm programming myself to accept madness.	It's wonderful, It's terrific, or It's fantastic
It's hellishly/infernally great! (for great experiences).	I'm programming myself to accept hellish situations in my life.	It's super great, It's fantastic …
I would like to go off on a vacation.	The conditional: I must detect what I fear if I get what I say I want. "I would like to" translates to: I want, but I'm afraid that....	I feel like going off on a vacation.
I would like to go off on a vacation.	"I would like to" translates to: I want to, but I think I'm not able to do it.	I want to go off on a vacation.

NEGATIVE Expression	Comments	POSITIVE Expression
It's **unbelievable**, what has just happened . . .	I don't believe what I've gone through, what I see or hear, I don't believe it, I put myself in a world of illusion; I program myself to not believe in anything real. It's a sort of escape from reality.	It's **fantastic**, what has just happened . . .
It's **not worth the trouble** to come and help me to . . .	I emphasize the trouble, the sadness in carrying out the actions of my life. . . . Everything is distressful.	It's OK like this, thanks for your offer, I can do it by myself. It's **no use** . . .
Does this **bother** you?	I don't take my place, I put myself in the position of who is unwanted, who disturbs, who must belittle oneself.	Does this suit you?
Don't you have a minute to give me?	With a negative question, I expect a negative answer, so I am not taking my place. Am I sure I'm only asking the other person for 1 minute and 0 second?	**Could you spare a few minutes** to give me?
To **wangle**, or **finagle** my way (out of a problem).	Focuses on the problem rather than the solution.	**To arrive at finding a solution**
I think	I think (mental), I believe (belief), or I **know** (integrated in myself). What is my position?	**I know**

NEGATIVE Expression	Comments	POSITIVE Expression
It's not bad	I'm programming myself in terms of bad.	It's good
It's terribly good! (for things that are great to enjoy).	I'm programming myself in terms of fear.	It's surprising. It's fantastic.
It's not terribly great		It's common, It's ordinary
It's unforgettable	Do I refer to forgetting because I have memory problems?	This will stay etched in my memory.
There is no obligation to . . .	I emphasize the constraints I'm imposing on myself	I am free to . . .
It's not possible to do it this way?	I close myself.	Is it possible to do it this way?
I stay blocked somehow.	I block myself, I freeze . . .	I must open myself more
I'm letting you go on	I don't care.	Do as you wish
I'm leaving you . . .	The idea is separation.	I'll stay in contact
You should . . .	The idea is constraint; I impose an idea, a way of doing things.	I suggest that you . . .
I should . . .		I could . . .
I am no good at this . . .	The idea is depreciation; I emphasize learning and improvement instead.	I'm distracted, I'll be more careful the next time.
I should have . . .	The idea is guilt; I emphasize learning and improvement instead.	I will do it differently the next time.

NEGATIVE Expression	Comments	POSITIVE Expression
I am distrustful	I emphasize distrust, the negative. I focus instead on what is going on and what can happen, good or not so good.	I am vigilant
That's not too Bad Nasty Evil Difficult Complicated Obscure Stupid	Negation of a negative notion; I program myself negatively.	It's Beautiful Good Benevolent Worthy Easy
You're not Incapable of . . . Without . . . On the street Poor		You're Intelligent Capable of . . . With . . . You have a roof over your head You have the means
I have constraints	Lack of ease and freedom	I am busy
I have work engagements	Heaviness	I have work
I don't have the choice	Lack of freedom before a number of choices available to me. I don't want to see all the choices. I limit myself for lack of freedom.	Among my many options, I have made the choice of . . .
I'm expecting your telephone jangle	Refers to shrill, violent sounds	I'm expecting your phone call
Is nobody there?	Solitude . . .	Is someone there?
Treatment	Medical officialese	Care, medicine, visit, cure

NEGATIVE Expression	Comments	POSITIVE Expression
I give myself treatments	I sound very distant from myself here	I take care of myself
There's no problem	Heaviness of tone	It's OK
It's bloody good	Do I really like things "bloody"?	It's very good
It's too good, It's excessively good	I thus limit myself in what is good; if I find It's too much, then it's too . . . I can never manifest more . . .	It's very, very good
I'm not worried	I emphasize worry . . .	I'm confident
No, No, everything's fine!	It's as if I were expecting reproaches or negative comments from the other person; so I pre-emptively attack first to foil the expected attack. But saying "no, no" reveals my lack of trust in the other person.	Yes, Yes, everything's fine!
Will it bother you if I . . . ?	I don't take my place. I'm bothersome . . . I also think for the other person . . .	Will it suit you if I...?
How are you doing? It's sort of OK I guess. We get by . . .	This is a form of complaint, sadness, a lack of energy and joy that I pump in the other person, a resistance to trust.	It's OK / or: It's not OK (Be clear and accurate).
For each pain its sorrow	Behind the pain I see only the sorrow or the sadness. Emphasize instead what I do with this experience and what I must understand from it.	For each pain I accept the lesson I must understand.

NEGATIVE Expression	Comments	POSITIVE Expression
I don't have the time.	We all have the same time. Saying this is totally false; I'm posing as a victim. What must be up front is how I use my time, the priorities I choose, and also the mastery of my life.	**I didn't take the time.** I have **other priorities.**
I haven't come **for nothing**	A sense of depreciation	I have come **for something**
The sun is **banging down**	Watch out for the fiery bangs!	The sun is **very hot**
Don't be afraid!	It's better to refer to confidence than to fear . . .	**Be confident!**
I'll have to, I must . . .	I treat things as constraints. I should instead emphasize the freedom I allow myself.	**I can** . . . It is **necessary** for me to . . .

The Power of "I"
in Positive Thoughts

The following sentences come from different books that I have used as references (see p. 121), but which have been modified to the "I" viewpoint or to a positive formulation. I can do this exercise by taking each sentence and **pronouncing it out loud with a hand on my heart ♥** to facilitate its integration.

It is important that I nourish my mind with positive sentences, if only to compensate for all the negative sentences I may say or hear during my day.

1. I am happy, always. Any path is easier to travel, any burden is lighter, any shadow over my **heart ♥** or in my mind dissipates faster for me, the person determined to be happy. (*Vivre dans l'enthousiasme*)

2. The fullness of life is free of external things. I, myself, must create beauty in my life. (*Comment réussir sa vie*)

3. **I am the source of my abundance.** (*Creating Money*)

4. What I must do, instead of looking at things stretching vaguely into the distance, is to do something that is close at hand. – Carlyle. (*The Greatest Secret in the World*)

5. I radiate self-esteem, inner peace, **love**, well-being, and happiness. (*Creating Money*)

6. If I am a man who has cultivated in myself the peace of God, then I remain calm through the little storms of life. (*Fais-toi confiance*)

7. Everything I create satisfies me fully. (*Creating Money*)

8. As a human being, I must directly **accept** ↓♥ the circumstances around me, and I have the power to choose my thoughts and, therefore, to form the circumstances of my life. (*As a Man Thinketh*)

9. I am in the right place at the right time. (*Creating Money*)

10. I must tend toward the accomplishment of my inner being, wherever prevails a deep desire to excel. (*Living with Enthusiasm*)

11. The only man who never makes a mistake is the one who never does anything. I feel responsible for my experiences, provided I don't make the same one twice. – Roosevelt (*The Law of Success*)

12. I savour the path traveled as well as the goal. (*Creating Money*)

13. Friendship is like life and **love**. I must support it and take care of it, or else it will deteriorate and disappear. (*Au cas où vous croiriez être normal*).

14. My beliefs determine my reality. I believe in my infinite prosperity. (*Creating Money*)

15. I fully live each day that passes. Each day is a new existence that will never return; I draw the best out of it. (*Conquest of Frustration*)

16. I allow myself to possess more than I believed possible. (*Creating Money*)

17. If I aim for the Sun, I may reach a star. – P.T. Barnum

18. I send **love** to my anguish. My fears are the parts of my being that expect my **love**. (*Creating Money*)

19. I don't expect success; **IT** expects me. When the opportunity knocks, I must open the door to it myself. (*The Miracle of Motivation*)

20. I am confident in the fact that everything happens at the ideal moment and in the ideal way. (*Creating Money*)

21. I keep in mind that happiness is the only product in the world that multiplies by dividing itself. (*Psycho-Cybernetics*)

22. I'll be on the road to success, as long as I don't say: "*I give up.*" (*Plus haut, toujours plus haut*)

23. I never stop working and playing because I'm getting old; I am ageing because I've stopped working and playing. (*Rendez-vous au sommet*)

24. My self-image is my **Conscience**. I make it clear and bright **now**. (*Psycho-Cybernetics*)

25. I forget the regrets of the past. I live in the present. I set goals for myself in the present. (*Conquest of Frustration*)

26. Everything I do brings more beauty, harmony, order, and **light** into the universe. (*Creating Money*)

27. I never say anything that I would not dare to write and sign. (*Les relations humaines*)

28. I discover what the most essential task of my existence is by gazing into myself rather than outward. (*Creating Money*)

29. The most practical, beautiful, the most "feasible" philosophy will do nothing if I don't do something. (*Rendez-vous au sommet*)

30. If I want to reach my goal, I must envision its trajectory in my mind before getting there. (*Rendez-vous au sommet*)

31. I am a precious person. My existence is important. (*Creating Money*)

32. I don't make a big deal out of nothing. I don't kill butterflies with a rifle. (*How to Live with Yourself*)

33. The worst decision of all is the one I haven't yet made. (*Rendez-vous au sommet*)

34. I **accept** ↓♥ myself and **love** myself for what I am at this exact moment. (*Creating Money*)

35. I fear nobody, I hate nobody, I wish no evil on anyone and more than probably, I will have many friends. (*The Law of Success*)

36. I think like a member of the crew and not like a passenger. (*La magie de s'auto-diriger*)

37. I invite the good to enter my life and I allow it to enter. (*Creating Money*)

38. I become what I think. (*The Greatest Miracle in the World*)

39. If I think about happiness, I will act like a happy person. Thought generates action. (*Arrêter la terre de tourner, je veux descendre*)

40. I let go, knowing that nothing will come of my life without something better showing up. (*Creating Money*)

41. It's what is in me that will make me advance. (*Rendez-vous au sommet*)

42. To leap out of this uncertain world, I need an inner strength that will set me on fire. (*Psycho-Cybernetics*)

43. It is by transforming myself that I transform the world around me. (*Creating Money*)

44. I enjoy this day **today**... And tomorrow's, tomorrow. (*The Greatest Miracle in the World*)

45. From now on, I remember that there are no limits to the achievement of my desires, all the way to the end of my days. (*It's Terrific!*)

46. I've failed several times? How lucky I am! Now I should know the things I should NOT do. (*The Law of Success*)

47. When I begin to know myself, I begin to live. (*Comment réussir sa vie)*

48. I know my worth and I respect it. (*Creating Money*)

49. In each one of us, there is greatness. I must **accept ↓♥** to see it. (*Conquest of Frustration*)

50. The quality of my life depends on my **attitude**. It depends on me whether everything is simple or complicated. (*Comment réussir sa vie*)

51. I appreciate everything I am and everything I possess. (*Creating Money*)

52. I remember that my true fortune can be assessed not by what I have, but by what I am. (*The Law of Success*)

53. Any problem that I can simplify to the point where I can state it clearly in a single sentence is already half-resolved. (*Conquest of Frustration*)

54. I never seek to be anything else but myself. (*The Greatest Success in the World*)

55. Everything I offer to others acknowledges and respects their value. (*Creating Money*)

56. As soon as I believe enough in something, it takes form in my mind, aroused by my inner creative force. (*Your Inner Strength – TNT*)

57. I must be able to live with myself before being able to live with someone else. (*How to Live with Yourself*)

58. I always try to make others win; when other people win, it's a success for myself. (*Creating Money*)

59. I act **according to** people and not **at their expense**. (*Les relations humaines*)

60. **Love** is a gift that I provide without asking for anything in return. (*The Greatest Miracle in the World*)

The Potent Power of Saying THANKS

Openness to Love and Acceptance ↓ ♥

Thank you, two small words that can make all the difference in my life when used. In French, it is interesting to note that the **word for "thank you"**

M-e-r-c-i

has the same number of letters as the **word** for "**love**"

A-m-o-u-r

In fact, every time I say **thank you**, I express my **love** to someone or for a situation. For example, when I say **thank you** to a waiter in a restaurant, I express my **love** for the service he has rendered. However, does the urge to say **thank you** come naturally after having a car accident, being fired, or learning that my partner is leaving me for someone else or that a loved one has unexpectedly died? I think there is a good chance the answer to this question will be *"No."* However, I need to learn how to see things differently! Why?

Understanding what follows is related to two basic principles. First, **I am 100 percent responsible for what I experience**. And second, **love is everywhere in the universe**, including any event that occurs in my life, whether I consider it good or bad. So, when I say **thank you** for a situation, even if it isn't obvious, I connect with the principle that says that everything that happens does so for a reason, whether I'm conscious of that reason or not. In addition, considering that **I become that which I focus my attention on**, I might as well focus my attention on **love** to reap the most benefits and to understand why it is happening. If I focus my attention on the fact that what I'm going through is disastrous, frightening, or terrible, well then . . .

I often say to participants in my workshops that when and if a brick falls on my head, I'll respond by saying **thank you**. I know it's not easy to understand and that it might seem masochistic, but in reality I'm not saying **thank you** to the suffering.

This exercise has to do with my higher self.

> *I say thank you because I know there is a reason for what is happening to me and that I need to become aware of something.*

That is why I'm saying **thank you**. We sometimes throw bricks in the air and forget about having done so, and, when they fall back down a month later, we don't remember and say: *"What have I done in my life to deserve this?"*

Incidentally, these events don't serve as punishment. It's simply the rule of cause and effect. If I insert my finger in an electrical outlet and get electrocuted, is it because God wanted to punish me?

It may seem bizarre sometimes when I use this technique, but I must say that, just like many others, I can feel the benefits almost immediately.

> ### The "THANK YOU" technique
> ### is part of an Acceptance ↓♥ technique,[8]
> ### because: I cannot change anything
> ### that I have not accepted ↓♥.

One day, I visited a woman who was bedridden at home because she suffered from terminal bone cancer. My relationship with her was very good. As her weekly exercise, I asked her to say **thank you** to her cancer many times during the day. She looked at me curiously and found it a bit ridiculous to do such a thing, but she knew inside that, even if she didn't understand why I was asking her to do this, there most certainly was a good reason to go along with my request.

In her case, the bone cancer was due to a profound lack of self-esteem. It followed an episode of breast cancer several years before that had required a mastectomy. The second bout of cancer was the result of psychological stress resulting from her lack of self-esteem, which in turn had been brought about partly by her breast cancer.

Unable to bear the situation, the brain chose to transform her psychological stress into biological stress and gave her a disease to help her survive longer. Without this transfer, she would have died much sooner. This is what she had to be **thankful** for. She needed **to thank her brain for having made the best decision, that of prolonging her life** and giving her enough time to find a solution and a cure. Of course, if no solution is found, this woman will die of bone cancer, but she will have lived longer thanks to the process the brain initiated. Something particular

---

8 See further explanation of the Acceptance technique in my book: *The 5 Steps to Achieve Healing*, Les Éditions ATMA Internationales (2014).

happens when I use this technique, something that has nothing to do with logic. Of course, it's not the first thing that would come to mind – to say thank you when a mishap occurs or when you're inconvenienced.

Since it doesn't involve logic, through this technique I bypass my mental blocks and connect more closely with intuition and **love**.

By looking at a situation or considering it from a superior point of view, i.e., from the perspective of my higher self, the perspective of the **Soul**, I access a privileged position. My basic assumption is that everything in the universe is **love** and exists for the best of my evolution. It's easier than to see and understand why the events that are occurring in my life are happening, and to **accept** ↓ ♥ them more readily.

> *I must learn to never stop saying "Thanks,"*
> *rather than asking.*

This is a quite extraordinary key. Indeed, when I **ask for** something, my subconscious takes it for granted that it is because I am **lacking** something. I can feel it at the level of my heart ♥ as an emptiness. Also, I am in the attitude of **expecting** results. There is a great likelihood that my ego is at the origin of this request.

When I **ask for** something, I put myself in a state for receiving. When I say **THANKS**, I put myself in a state for giving.

However, if I want to receive or to have something in my life, I can get around the difficulty by formulating my request as follows:

> *THANK YOU from all my being*
> *for giving me THAT.*

I thus put more into action the principle that I am related to the abundance that exists in the universe and that it is accessible to me Here and Now. I am only being grateful for what I already know has been granted to me by divine right. Saying **THANK YOU** helps me develop my power of gratitude.

> *The more I say "THANK YOU," the more*
> *my power of gratitude increases and*
> *the more my heart ♥ opens up.*

Thus, the more my power of gratitude grows within me, the more I will attract gratitude in my life with the people I mix with or the events that surround me.

Personally, I practice that with the situations around me. I sometimes say:

thank you to those who laid down the asphalt that enables me to drive more smoothly on the road;

thank you to those who set up the streetlights along the side of the road, because it makes my driving safer;

thank you to the birds and their songs that help cheer up my day;

thank you to the flowers I find along my way and that brighten my life;

thank you to those who set up the road signs along the road, for it enables me to find my way more easily;

thank you to those who contributed to build the Samuel de Champlain Promenade in Quebec City, this marvellous park bordering the majestic St Lawrence River;

thank you to Napoleon and to the people who, in his time, planted all those trees along the edges of the Canal du Midi in the South of France and along several highways in France, so that I find myself in an enchanting scenery;

thank you to those who installed the elevator where I now find myself because it enables me to avoid climbing interminable stairs and to reach my appointment more quickly;

thank you to Louis XIV and the thousands of workers and conservationists who now allow me to admire this splendid place called the Château de Versailles.

Thank You!
Thank You!
Thank You!

If, for any reason at all, I happen to feel a little morose, I can practice this exercise of saying **THANK YOU** to increase my gratitude towards Life and thus dissipate all those shortages in which my mind tries to make me believe.

So, when I say THANK YOU, instead of drawing attention to myself, I turn it outward and towards the entire universe. I thus apply the following assertion:

The more I give the more I receive!

I may be a little reluctant to say **THANK YOU**. This may derive from the fact that when I perform an action that tends to open my heart ♥, there is a memory that rears up, sometimes unconsciously, and reminds me that several times in the past, when I've opened my heart ♥, I have been wounded. So, when I feel the danger of opening it up **again**, it is important that I get beyond this fear, however unconscious, to reach for more Wisdom, more **Love** and more Freedom.

The True Power of Integration and Healing from Saying THANK YOU

In the book *The 5 Steps to Achieve Healing*, these five steps are discussed in more detail:

> *Knowledge*
>
> *Openness*
>
> *Letting go*
>
> *Acceptance* ↓♥
>
> *Action*

When I say **THANK YOU** and thus open my heart ♥, I enter the process of acceptance ↓♥ that leads me to healing and the opening of **Consciousness** that goes with it. This process does not function according to logic, but it is most effective, as I have been able to observe its results.

In June 2011, I gave a *Finding My Inner Child* workshop in Quebec, Canada. Among the 16 participants, there was a woman, whom I shall call Denise, in her late fifties, who had been sexually abused by her father from the age of two or three.

During the workshop, at the moment when she was sharing with my assistant what she had experienced between the ages of nine months and three years, her body had some psychosomatic reactions and recalled the events to the point that she felt herself choking up and reliving the scene where her father was thrusting his penis into her mouth, etc. Denise had done at least five years of therapy, she had a Ph.D. in psychology, but this situation with her father was still not resolved. She knew the principle that was discussed in the workshop, namely that: **I am 100 percent**

responsible for everything that happens to me, whatever my age, and that:

> Everything that happens is intended
> for a raising of Consciousness,
> so that I may find myself with more Love,
> more Wisdom, and more Freedom.

I then asked her to turn her attention on all the times she had been abused by her father and then, while looking me in the eyes, to say **THANK YOU**, again and again, at least 20 to 30 times, slowly, so that she could feel the impact of the words as strongly as possible in her heart ♥. Of course, she first felt anger and then refusal and annoyance, before at last seeing the emergence of more calm and inner peace. This exercise enabled her to understand in her heart ♥, and not in her head, why that had happened to her. And at the end of the workshop, she was able to share with us that, for the first time in her life, she could now say: "*I love you, Papa . . .*" Wasn't that a beautiful liberation?

> I know that what I experience is meant
> to bring more Love, Freedom and
> Wisdom into my life.

FOR SMOKING

I have started asking those participants in my workshops who are smokers to go for a cigarette during the breaks and to say **thank you** every time they inhale the smoke from their cigarette. The results are sometimes quite immediate. In fact, some individuals who do the exercise correctly can't even finish their cigarette because they feel nauseous. This can be an inexpensive way to quit smoking. Recently, a friend who knew the technique smoked three cigarettes in a row, saying **thank you** every time she inhaled. The nausea was so intense while doing this that she was able to start the withdrawal process.

FOR EATING

I told a person who wanted to eat less to say **thank you** every time she swallowed food. During the first meal following the exercise, she felt that it was working and that she wasn't so hungry. She was full and didn't need to finish her plate. This really encouraged her to start the diet she had planned.

IN GENERAL

It is sufficient to say **thank you** to anything that bothers me **without trying to understand,** because **it helps to keep my heart ♥ open and integrate situations to change them.** When I'm on the road, I sometimes say **thank you** in my heart to those who paved it, put up the lampposts, the road signs, planted the trees, and so on. I could tell myself that, after all, they were paid to do the job. Of course they were! But someone still had to do the job and that is why I say **thank you**.

I would say that whatever happens in life, it's important to say **thank you** because it reduces my stress and increases my chances of staying healthy.

I was personally confronted with this on my first trip to Switzerland. The person whose place I was living in decided, overnight, to literally throw me out the door without any explanation. I found myself alone in the street with my luggage and I had to get to the train station in this small town that was about a kilometre away. I told myself that the homeless were better off than me because at least they had carts to carry their things in.

Once I got to the station in Geneva, with all my luggage next to me, someone drew my attention over to the right and asked for some information in a language I didn't understand. A few seconds later, I realized someone else had just stolen the bag that contained my new laptop computer, my portable printer, and a few other items, all in all worth 5,300 Euro.[9] I had had enough for one day and was even starting to think that it was too much. However, my inner voice cautioned me. It told me to be careful not to **build up any overload of stress** because, depending on how my brain would interpret it, I could develop an illness.

I had been **aware** of this for a couple of years and so, without much enthusiasm, but wanting to send information to my brain, I started **looking at the positive side** of what had just happened: "*Consider this, Jacques,*" I told myself. "*You have one less bag to carry. Anyway, that bag would have been cumbersome on*

---

9   Equivalent to approximately CA $ 7,400 or US $ 6,700 back then.

the subway in Paris. Your laptop and the rest of the stuff can be replaced. Ninety-five percent of the data in your laptop is in your computer at home anyway and you are probably insured for theft. You can check when you get home. Really, it's only a theft . . . It could have been much worse. You could have had an accident and ended up in the hospital." I also recalled the catastrophe that had occurred on the funicular in the old city in Quebec a few months before, where some tourists were badly hurt, and others died.

Despite being bothered by the theft of my bag following the incident earlier in the day, it was important for my brain to register useful information that would allow it to reduce the level of my stress. Would the stress I was experiencing have been sufficient to trigger an illness? I can't say, but I was better off putting all odds on my side for it not to happen, and that's why I said **thank you** even though I didn't really understand why things were happening to me. I knew it was the best I could do. And so, I've learned to say **thank you** as often as I can, and my life is so much better.

Thus, when a situation disturbs me and makes me experience frustration, I hasten to say **THANKS**, even if I say it through clenched teeth, because my brain registers it too, and I even also add: "*It's marvelous, it's fantastic, it's extraordinary.*" Now imagine that I have a small accident with my car. So, I say: "*THANKS, it's marvellous, it's fantastic, it's extraordinary.*" This may not seem logical, but the principle involved here is that I am 100 percent responsible for everything that happens to me, even if technically someone else may be in the wrong. The **THANKS** leads me to remain in an attitude of openness rather than closing myself off and resigning myself to be fatalistic, and thus become better **conscious** of why it happened to me and show acceptance ↓ ♥ and illustrate the principle that: **There is nothing I can change that I have not first accepted** ↓ ♥.[10]

When I add: *It's marvellous, it's fantastic, it's extraordinary*, it is simply to draw my attention to something positive instead of resenting the situation and thus putting negative energy on that situation.

For the **Soul** that I am, and this is true for any one of us, EVERYTHING that happens to me is only made up of EXPERIENCES, whether these are considered by me, as a human being, as positive or negative. Whether I win at the Lotto or my house goes up in flames, these are only two different experiences for the **Soul**. However, it remains true that I may have a preference between the two.

Here are some examples of notes sent by someone to their lover using the **THANK YOU Technique**:

Thank you for the mail you send me, it makes me happy.
Thank you for your phone call, it calms me.
Thank you for your openness, it puts more **light** into my life.

---

10 See more explanations on this subject in the book: *The 5 Steps to Achieve Healing.*

Thank you for being nice, it brings me joy.

Thank you for being understanding, it comforts me.

Thank you for your tenderness, it warms my heart ♥.

Thank you for having confidence in me, it reassures me.

Thank you for your **love**, it helps me grow.

Thank you for your smile, it increases my hope in life.

Thank you for the time you spend with me, I feel more **love** inside me.

Thank you for those long kisses where I lose myself but stay connected to you.

Thank you for your caresses that make me more accepting ↓ ♥ of myself in this world.

Thank you for letting me caress you, it gives me an opportunity to be in contact with **love** in this world.

Thank you for enjoying pleasure with me, I can benefit from the openness of the moment.

Thank you for embracing my body; it helps me to accept ↓ ♥ more deeply that I'm part of this world.

Thank you!

Thank you!

Thank you!

⌒

TESTIMONIAL

After giving a massage, I asked my client what she experienced during the session. She answered that, compared to the other times, this session had been better for her. She had felt more openness, which had enabled her to let go of more things and with much more ease.

During the whole massage, I had repeated the mantra: Thank you, Thank you, Thank you.

Repeating this mantra is as effective in acupressure. The impact on each point is quite immediate.

I tried the experiment again on another client and I understood that it was particularly beneficial when she told me at the end of the session that during the massage, while I was repeating THANK YOU, she was repeating "I accept↓♥, I accept↓♥ to open myself, I accept↓♥ more openness, always."

— Danièle F., November 2002

PARTICIPANTS' COMMENTS

Saying THANK YOU is both a very simple and effective tool. I've noticed that when I'm in a situation that disturbs me, saying THANK YOU allows me to deactivate a negative reaction before judging. I sense that my heart♥ remains more open and it reduces my level of stress. It's as if I were telling myself: "No use getting nervous or reacting, try to see why it's happening!"

Saying THANK YOU helps me to remain in acceptance↓♥ of what is happening, even if it appears to be negative. I often say THANK YOU in positive situations when good things happen to me. When I do this, a feeling of abundance overcomes me. I accentuate the positive. Everything seems to be even more beautiful!

— *L.B.*

I often say THANK YOU when I face a problem. For example, when a client takes ages to pay a bill or when a neighbor irritates me.

It's a good opportunity to work on myself. Saying THANK YOU becomes beneficial for me, and I develop a positive attitude in all aspects.

— *J.D.*

I try to think about this technique as often as possible to say THANK YOU and to remain open. It's not an automatic reflex yet! Truly, it's a technique that helps us manage our emotional reactions and enables us to be more serene and avoid panicking in the face of adversity. THANK YOU!

— *V.R.*

I use the THANK YOU exercise very often, and I sometimes repeat it as a mantra. It helps me to overcome everyday situations that bother me, like when I'm driving, at the supermarket, on a train, or whatever it may be. It helps me to defuse my anger, to avoid criticizing or to let negative thoughts enter my mind. Used as a mantra, it helps me to regain my calmness when a situation has disturbed me.

I also repeat it very often for the good things the universe and Life bring me. I say THANK YOU for my food, for my house, my family, etc. I'm thankful. It fulfills me while helping me to be more tolerant.

— *C.L.*

It's a very practical and efficient technique that helps me to refocus on my rules of humanistic behavior and to objectively put things in perspective.

— *J-L.P.*

This technique helps us to accept↓♥ with love any situation, even the most difficult ones. I do the exercise more and more often daily, in my emotional and professional life. It goes from saying THANK YOU for simply not falling over to THANK YOU for not being in a car accident. I also say THANK YOU more often for those small and big joys life brings, like my partner's tender gestures. I also simply say THANK YOU to LIFE. It has become a natural reflex to give THANKS for those happy moments in my life.

Of course, it's not as automatic when I live through difficult situations! It's harder to say THANK YOU when events are negative. But since attending that workshop in Carcassonne, I know I can transmute lead into gold and more importantly I know how to do it! It will help me to say THANK YOU under ANY AND ALL CIRCUMSTANCES.

— *H.N.*

This technique is simply wonderful!! I've tried it out many times.

When something bothers me, if I hear something that I don't like, I say THANK YOU in an automatic way because I know there is a reason behind it.

Recently, I badly hurt my finger. The pain was intense, and I heard myself saying THANK YOU in my head. I was really surprised to see to what extent it had become instinctive. So, I repeated again and again THANK YOU as a mantra. I was in great pain, but I knew there was a reason for it. What's funny is that I really didn't feel like saying THANK YOU for I was angry at the pain, but I forced myself to repeat THANK YOU, THANK YOU, THANK YOU. When I calmed down and the pain subsided, I went to look up the symbolic meaning of hurting a finger in *The Encyclopedia of Ailments and Diseases*. Well, what I read matched exactly what I was experiencing at the moment, and I understood why I was saying THANK YOU!

— *M.L.*

Automatic Acceptance
through Deleting the "NOs"

Indeed, I may often give a comment or a reply to a question by starting my sentence with a "NO." For instance, when a person asks me something and I answer:

"NO," I'm interested,	change to	"YES," I am interested.
"NO," I'll think about it,	change to	"YES," I'll think about it.
"NO," I want to tell you ...	change to	"YES," I want to tell you ...

It's impressive, the number of "**NOs**" that a person can say in a few minutes and that the brain registers. I think about the high number of "**NOs**" that my brain registers in a single day. I notice that I say "**NO**" mostly when I'm about to say something that will make me show more openness, and that fits the explanation given above, namely that I am about to open myself more and my memory has registered that in the past, when I opened myself, it put me in danger or hurt me inside. Thus, unconsciously, I try to limit my openness to feel more secure. It is therefore important for me to practice replacing the "**NOs**" with "YESs."

The Importance of the Words "Always" and "Never"

I have mentioned that my brain operates like a computer, which explains the importance of **words**, their meaning and their conscious or unconscious programming inside of me.

> *When I use the words "ALWAYS" or "NEVER," it involves the principle of ETERNITY.*

Therefore, I must be vigilant when I use these two **words**. If I say, for example: "*I'm always losing my keys,*" it means that I lose my keys ten times out of ten, for all **eternity**. Maybe I lose them often, or even very often, but that is different from "**always.**" If in fact I lose my keys eight times out of ten, then I have just programmed my brain to lose them all the time, namely ten times out of ten.

Similarly, if I say: "*I'm never lucky at the lottery,*" even if my level of success is low, I have just programmed myself to reduce it to 0 percent to conform to what my brain has just heard.

And every time I won't have won, I will reinforce this situation by saying "*I just knew it,*" which will reinforce this "truth" even more in my brain.

However, I can use these two **words** to my advantage if I say, for example:

*I know I am **always** guided and protected.*

*I will **always** have the necessary money I need to advance my projects.*

*I love you **forever**.*

***Never** will anyone be able to exert on me an influence that could be negative.*

The Healing Words of the Book
The Encyclopedia of Ailments and Diseases

A French former physician, Mr Gérard Athias,[11] noticed during his examinations of patients that when he was able to have his patient say a **word** derived from the etymological root of the name of the sickness, it sometimes gave rise to an emotion that could set off a healing process.

In fact, the brain **"knows"** that the two words are interrelated, but it may not be **aware** of this. I will therefore go through the back door to get inside the house, namely the conflict and/or the emotion related to it, then free this emotion or show some understanding to enable the healing to take place.

This explanation is not given in the book *The Encyclopedia of Ailments and Diseases,* but I can still identify these **words** based on the etymological root of the name of the disease by looking up the words that are printed in a ***bold italic*** typeface.

These words were taken during a workshop led by Gérard Athias in which he explained this procedure. With his permission, these words were incorporated into the text of the book *The Encyclopedia of Ailments and Diseases* to describe the metaphysical approach of ailments and diseases by placing them in an appropriate sentence. It is sometimes a way to catch an emotion related to the conflict without the mind being **aware**

---

11 Website: www.athias.net

of it. I call this "going in through the back door." In fact, my conscious mind does not necessarily associate the **word** with its link to the disease, and chances are that it will have repercussions and raise emotions in a process of liberation and healing. That is why those **words** *in bold italic* type are important, especially in the **monosyllabic pronunciation exercise** described in this book. I will then have a better chance of activating the emotions that are at the root of my conflict.

The Healing of Monosyllabic Pronunciation

This technique is an integration technique that enables me to heal injuries at their source by using the alchemical power of the heart ♥ to effect the transformation. It is a powerful technique that is proven.

This section is an excerpt taken from *The Encyclopedia of Ailments and Diseases*:

The Integration through Monosyllabic, Rhythmic, and Sequential PronounciationTechnique

One can use the information from this book to bring about change at the emotional level. The following exercise helps to activate one's emotional memory. It enables part of the emotions, moving from head to heart ♥, to be healed in **love**.

It involves reading a text that describes feelings of uneasiness or an illness, syllable by syllable, and taking at least one second per syllable as you read.

For instance, let's take the following condition: arthritis.

Arthritis (In General)

Arthritis is defined as inflammation of the joints. It can affect any part of the human locomotive system, be it bone, ligament, tendon, or muscle. Its characteristics are inflammation of the joints, stiffness of the muscles, and pain, and it is associated on a metaphysical level with lack of openness, being judgemental, affliction, sadness, or anger.

Becomes:

Ar-thri-tis (In-Ge-ne-ral)

Ar-thri-tis-is-de-fined-as-in-flam-ma-tion-of-the-joints.-It-can-af-fect-a-ny-part-of-the-hu-man-lo-co-mo-tion-sys-tem-be-it-bone,-li-ga-ment,-ten-don-or-mus-cle.-Its-cha-rac-ter-is-tics-are-in-flam-ma-tion-of-the-joints,-stiff-ness-of-the-mus-cles-and-pain,-and-it-is-as-so-ci-a-ted-on-a-me-ta-phy-si-cal-le-vel-with-lack-of-o-pen-ness,-be-ing-judge-men-tal,-af-flic-tion,-sad-ness-or-an-ger.

And I continue reading the text in this way right to the end. It's important to read very slowly, **no faster than one second per syllable and even slower if possible**. It doesn't matter whether the intellect understands the **words** or not, or the sentences that are being read. Feelings of sadness may surface during the exercise. If so, simply put **love** into the situation.

I can use a text describing the sickness I'm currently suffering from, an illness I came down with in the past, or one I am afraid of contracting. If I experience some emotion during the exercise, I can repeat it later on, until I no longer feel anything disturbing while doing it and am more at ease with the text.

If I want, I can do this exercise after meditation or after listening to some quiet music or following a relaxation session. I can also do the exercise using the preface or the introduction from *The Encyclopedia of Ailments and Diseases.*

The following instructions will further explain how to use this integration technique. To begin with, again let me explain that, from my perspective, **integration** means to become **conscious** of oneself and, to some extent, it also means **healing**. Indeed, an ailment or sickness is but a message from the body meant to raise **awareness** on what is currently occurring in one's life.

I first used this technique in a workshop I've been giving since March 1993 entitled *Recovering My Inner Child*. I apply it to the part of the workshop where the adult writes a letter to his inner child and the child writes back.

What happens when we do this exercise? First, you need to know that the faster one reads, the more the process of reading is a mental one. Similarly, the slower I read, the more what I am reading connects me with the energy centre (chakra) of the heart ♥.

> **Any ailment or disease**
> **is a conscious or unconscious**
> **interpretation of a lack of Love**
> **in relation to a situation or a person.**

It is as if this message or even this injury were registered at **love's** level, which in turn is associated in human beings on an energetic level with the heart ♥ chakra.

My wounds due to a lack of **love** are registered in the heart ♥ as some form of:

> **Rejection**
> **Abandonment**
> **Anger**

> Lack of understanding
> Sadness
> Disappointment
> and so forth.

These injuries may originate from one of the **six fundamental fears,**[12] **which are:**

> The fear of dying
> The fear of criticism
> The fear of sickness
> The fear of ageing
> The fear of poverty
> The fear of losing someone's Love.

To change the message that is registered inside me, **I must activate the information at its point of entry.** This means that in order to identify the situations that reactivate the emotions, I need to become **aware** of the "file" responsible for the information at the time it was entered, and I need to know the context regarding the origin of the injury when it happened. When recreating the circumstances that hurt, angered, or saddened me and so on, I open the heart ♥ chakra and, as a result, the chakra enables the healing energy of **love** to penetrate as well as **awareness.**

---

12 *The Law of Success*, Napoleon Hill. More explanations are also given in the book *The 5 Steps to Achieve Healing*, Jacques Martel, Les Éditions ATMA Internationales.

For the pronunciation exercise to be more effective, I imagine that my words come out of my heart ♥ as if my mouth was located in the heart ♥ chakra. During the exercise, tingling sensations or streams of warmth go through different parts of my body. Feelings of pain, sadness, and all kinds of emotions may occur. I try to remain calm when intense feelings of pain or sadness surface. It's a normal phenomenon and the body knows it can cope with it.

If for one reason or another I'm worried about experiencing too much emotion, I can do the exercise in the presence of someone who is able to support me in this process, someone responsible, like a therapist, for instance. I can apply this exceptional technique to many everyday situations.

I've been using this technique for several years in the *Recovering My Inner Child* workshop, where the adult is writing to their inner child and the child is writing back. The results are stunning. The participants experience unpredictable emotions in relation to different aspects of their lives.

Writing a Letter to Someone Close

First, you need to write the letter in positive terms in order to tone down its potentially negative impact on the person receiving it. That person's fears may surface, and he or she might feel guilty or blamed if this work isn't done. Rewriting a letter using positive wording involves choosing **words** or sentences that, without changing the meaning of the letter, are written in a positive overtone. For example, the following sentence: "*We never lacked anything*" becomes "*We always had what we needed.*" Once completed, the letter is read in monosyllabic form as explained previously.

However, I can do the monosyllabic reading exercise by reading the letter with negative formulations, but that is not the letter I will give here. I have often found that, for integration to take place, there are better results when some of the formulations are negative than when there are only positive formulations. Often, the "psychic weight" of the negative formulations is more important than the "psychic weight" of the positive formulations. And as the alchemy of the heart ♥ **always** transforms what goes through it into something positive, then there is often more material, or expressed emotions, in the negative, which will become positive, than in the positive itself.

Writing a Letter to Someone Who Has Passed On

Yes, it's possible! All I have to do is write down what I want to say or what I would have liked to have said to that person without considering any positive or negative aspects. I can write about how much I miss or loved them. Here is an example: "*The love I felt for you filled me with happiness all throughout those years and I miss it so very much. You were my sunshine and my hope in life . . .*"

If I encountered difficult times with the person and never had the opportunity to talk about it, I can write a letter. For example, if I were sexually abused and was deeply affected by it, I could write something like: "*You're just a disgusting and contemptible man. My life was completely disrupted because of you. I wanted to kill you hundreds of times . . .*" Interestingly, the transformation will happen in the heart ♥, even if the words are harsh and negative. However, it does happen sometimes that emotions surface.

Once the letter is written, I read it **syl-la-ble-by-syl-la-ble**, following the method explained previously, until the emotions surfacing are no longer intense. Then, I put the letter in an envelope, write the deceased person's last known address as well as the sender's address on it, and stick a stamp on it.

One day, a client in a therapy session with me couldn't stop saying how the stamp wasn't important. I put an end to the discussion by telling him that if the stamp wasn't important, then why didn't he simply stop arguing about it and stick it on the envelope.

Once the letter is ready to mail, I find a safe place where I can burn it. While it's burning, I visualize a white **light** coming down from the sky, like a laser beam, and entering my body through the top of my head, through my crown chakra, and reaching my heart ♥ and the burning letter. I concentrate on feeling the **love** moving inside me.

In reality, I've just sent my letter through "cosmic mail." It will be delivered on another vibratory plane. This technique has had interesting results for many people. I put the rational aspect of it all on hold and rely on the **Power of Love** that guides and heals me.

For Any Life Circumstance

I simply write down the situation I'm going through with a person, several individuals or with regards to a problem or malaise I'm having, and then I read the text **syl-la-ble-by-syl-la-ble, taking at least a second per syllable.**

For Spiritual Texts

I use spiritual texts taken from the Bible, psalms, and prayers to the saints or to my spiritual master, invocations, and so on and I read them monosyllabically.

PARTICIPANTS' COMMENTS

This technique truly enables me to bring up emotions that are deep inside of me. If I read rapidly, I actually sense the process as being a mental one. Reading it very slowly forces me to work from the heart♥, where some words vibrate more strongly than others and I realize that they carry an emotional charge. I have realized that this exercise is especially effective for writing letters that raise unpleasant issues with people whom I love. It enables me to be more neutral and to develop a more positive understanding of the things I'm writing about.

I have also tried this technique using *The Encyclopedia of Ailments and Diseases*. I realized that I was carrying emotions that were likely to make me sick – for instance developing multiple sclerosis – if I didn't deal with them appropriately and if I experienced great stress. It's as if my body had awakened upon reading specific words. I was able to see that I was heading towards having every emotional condition required to develop M.S. I read and reread the text until I no longer felt any emotion.

Upon my first reading, images surfaced as clues pointing to the origin of my uneasiness. It's as if when I do the exercise my heart connects directly to my emotional memory and does a quick search to find the information I need to become fully aware of what's happening and specially to deactivate and dissolve negative emotions.

— L.B.

I used this technique and found it very effective.
At one point in my life, I faced choices regarding my education and I wasn't sure if I should continue with university. So I wrote down on a piece of paper what I didn't like about pursuing my studies as well as the positive points of continuing my studies.

Having done this, I read the whole page syllable by syllable. Emotions welled up and then, in the next few days, I made the decision I felt was best for me at that time.

What changed by having done the exercise was that before reading the page I felt uncertainty and after reading it everything became clear.

Either way, I needed to make a decision, but I really wanted it to be in tune with what I was feeling. The monosyllabic pronunciation technique enabled this.

— M.L.

The Power of Words
in Guided Relaxation

Guided relaxation sessions, or directed relaxation sessions, are an interesting tool for me, "me" meaning here each one of us. In fact, as we live in a Western context, I haven't really learned to do meditation or contemplation exercises. Guided relaxation sessions enable me specially to make contact with the subconscious and to find answers to the questions that I ask myself.

> *They enable me to set off a process of opening up and healing.*

Understanding **guided relaxation sessions** can help us grasp the meaning of dreams. Indeed, they enable me to develop a method for operating at the subconscious level that can make it easier to understand. They enable us to create reference outlines that can be used by the subconscious to send us a message.

A Code of Ethics to Follow

It is important to understand that guided relaxation sessions are a powerful way to enter communication with the subconscious. I know the old axiom: "There are always two sides to a medal." For example, I know that money as such is neither positive nor negative; all depends on the use I make of it. Thus, **guided relaxation**

sessions represent a powerful means for reprogramming, to some extent, the subconscious. The programming can be positive or negative because the subconscious acts like a computer: it can't tell the difference.

The Functioning of Thought

A) My subconscious registers all the information and indexes it so that it can later refer to it.

B) My subconscious cannot tell the difference between the truth and fiction.

C) It also cannot tell the difference between what is real, imaginary, virtual, or symbolic.[13]

Positive Formulations

When suggestions are made to the subconscious, it is very important to use **only positive formulations**. The subconscious receives to different degrees a large part of everything it hears or sees. That is my reason for using positive formulations during workshops.

Negative formulations, even if they are neutralized by a denial, can have a negative impact. Here is an example of a negative formulation:

"I dive into the water. I am not afraid of drowning, and I feel perfectly comfortable."

In this formulation, it is important to note the presence of certain words: *"... AM ... AFRAID OF DROWNING..."* This may provoke a reaction and activate a fear, even unconscious, in a person.

---

13 These aspects are further developed in the book *The 5 Steps to Achieve Healing*, Les Éditions ATMA Internationales (2018).

How Does the Mind Respond to Fear?

- The fears are registered in the subconscious.
- The subconscious cannot tell the difference between reality and fiction.
- The subconscious can only act. It does not think.
- The fears and doubts suggest indirectly to the subconscious that they will actually come about.

Now here is the **positive formulation** of the same example:

"At the moment when I dive into the water, I already feel joy inside and I feel perfectly comfortable."

Some persons may be afraid of "diving into the water." By suggesting that *"AT THE MOMENT WHEN I DIVE, I ALREADY FEEL JOY INSIDE,"* I greatly diminish the risks of provoking a reaction. The same precautions must be taken when I do a guided relaxation session in which participants are invited to imagine themselves "in space," or in any situation where I lose my points of reference, which could make fear rise in me.

Relaxing the Body

There are many ways to relax the body. It depends on how much time or how much importance I want to give to relaxation.

I want you to benefit from my personal experience with **guided relaxation sessions**. Other people do things differently, but I can assure you that this method works. In any case, I am free to find out which one suits me best.

For example, during the relaxation session there are several ways to involve the different parts of the body. I can use more or fewer details.

1. General description:

*"I completely relax my two feet . . ., my two legs . . .,
I feel my two feet and my two legs completely relaxed."*

2. More detailed description:

*"I completely relax my toes, the soles of my feet, my heels,
and my ankles. Now I feel my two feet completely relaxed.
I also relax my calves, my knees and my thighs to feel my
two feet and my two legs perfectly relaxed . . ."*

3. A more detailed description and the metaphysical approach:

*"I completely relax my toes and I accept ↓♥ the details of
the future. I relax the soles of my feet and my heels, and
I accept ↓♥ the new directions of the future. I relax the
ankles and I accept ↓♥ to remain flexible with the new
directions of the future. I relax my calves, my knees and my
thighs and I gradually **accept** ↓♥ to go forward in life . . ."*

NOTE: I prefer to use expressions such as "I relax my arm . . ."
and "I feel my arm **lighter** and **lighter**" instead of "I feel my arm
heavier and **heavier**." I currently have no precise explanation to
offer to justify this choice, but I am more comfortable with these
expressions. I know that one then "manifests" a more natural situation for the body and the **conscience**.[14]

---

14 This can be compared with an excerpt from *Letters About Yoga*, by Sri
Aurobindo: «The descent of a higher **Conscience** into the more physical level
brings **light**, **Conscience**, strength and joy into the cells and all the physical
movements. The body becomes conscious and vigilant and it carries out
movements properly, obeying a higher will or automatically by the force of
the **Consciousness** that has descended into him. (. . .) It becomes possible
to reduce fatigue. Peace, joy, strength and **lightness** settle into the whole
physical system.

Using the "I" Instead of the "You"

Some people use the "You" in their relaxation sessions. Here is an example:

"You find yourself on a beach where you feel marvelously well. You feel the fine sand under your feet, and the sun is warming your whole body . . ."

As I noted above, this formulation can induce a psychological distance between the workshop leader and the participant. It may work, but the participant must listen to the leader "from the outside."

For my part, I prefer to use a formulation that enables me to feel engaged with the participant and that allows them to hear me "from inside." Thus, the previous example could be reformulated as follows:

"I find myself on a beach where I feel marvelously well. I feel the fine sand under my feet, and the sun is warming my whole body . . ."

Here, the participant hears the suggestion and **owns it,** without needing to "translate" what is heard, namely to change "You find yourself on a beach" for "I find myself on a beach." I can try out either one of the formulations and draw my own conclusions.

The Use of Superlatives and Other Terms to Reinforce Suggestion

Superlatives tend to increase the impact of "suggestion." For example, there is a difference between saying: "I feel quite well" and saying: "I feel marvelously well." Indeed, the second suggestion is more intense and enables me to act more strongly on the emotions. It enables me to **activate the emotional memory and therefore to bring about maximum changes.**

The Importance of "Open" Formulations

In order to give more **freedom** to the participant, it is important to use "**open**" formulations that make room for the participant. This way, the participant can add some information concerning their **individuality.**

Here is an example of a formulation I would describe as "**closed**":

> " . . . *I am standing before a <u>grey stone</u> cavern with <u>an entrance two metres high and one metre and a half wide.</u> A sage is there waiting for me. <u>He stands one metre seventy tall and has white hair and a white beard fifteen centimetres long. He is wearing a brown robe</u> that reaches to the ground and is drawn in at the waist by a yellow cord. <u>His sandals are dark brown. His eyes are blue</u> . . .* "

In this example, too many very precise details (<u>they are underlined</u>) can block or hinder the participant's personal vision.

Thus, the example could be reformulated more "openly":

> " . . . *I am standing before a cavern. I carefully note how it is made as well as its entrance. How high and wide it is. In front of the entrance, a sage is waiting for me. I carefully examine him: his hair, his height, his clothing, his piercing gaze, the impression he gives* . . . "

This formulation gives the participant (or their subconscious) the opportunity to "manifest" the characteristics of the cavern, the entrance, the sage (his age is not mentioned, though it may sometimes be added that he is "old"), his physical stature, his clothing, etc.

The details that manifest themselves to the participant can be revealing of what they are experiencing while meditating, or of certain conceptual insights experienced in the present instant. It is possible that certain aspects of these insights may change in the weeks and months following the meditation, depending on the leaps of **Consciousness** made by the participant.

The Power of Mantras
and Their Effects

A mantra is a sentence, a **word**, or a sound charged with spiritual power. It was originally an expression of the intuition arising from the depths of the **Soul** or the being. Repeating a mantra creates vibrations in the inner **Consciousness** that will prepare it to implement what the mantra symbolizes and is supposed to carry within itself. The mantra can become something that, consciously but spontaneously repeated in the very substance of **Consciousness**, no longer requires any mental effort.

A mantra is based on the power of sound. It is by the vibration of a sound and its resonance that a sound transforms its environment and the people reciting it. As the mantra is repeated many times in order to produce an effect, it therefore introduces the notions of cycle and repetition. Although mantras are often related to Hinduism and Buddhism, they are not linked to any language, culture, or animal species. At its most essential, **a mantra is a sound that produces a beneficial effect.**

The root of the **word** "mantra" originates from the Sanskrit and means **"the thought that frees and protects."** When I chant or recite a mantra, it activates or accelerates the creative spiritual force that is in me, inducing harmony in all the parts of my being. By the principle that **"I become that on which I focus my attention,"** this connects me more closely to higher spiritual energies and enables me to obtain a greater power for my own benefit and that of other people.

A **mantra** is not a prayer. A prayer consists of **words** of supplication chosen by a spiritual aspirant, whereas a **mantra** is a precise combination of **words** and **sounds** that lead me to a certain form of **Consciousness**. In fact, the **mantra** belongs to no religion. It is simply a sound that creates vibrations to open up **Consciousness** or to produce specific effects in any one of my bodies of energy.

I may tend to believe that when I chant a **mantra**, the sound originates from my throat. This is partly true, but I must remember that my body is made up of about 70 percent water and that a part of this water is vibrating too, and water is an excellent conductor of sound. I think of dolphins and whales communicating through water. Maybe even more important is that my larynx is supported by my spine and makes my skull bones vibrate along with all the bones in my spine, which **play the role of a harp tuned to the sounds of the universe**. It is my intention that makes all the parts of my being, spiritual and material, come together in harmony in order to manifest the intended state of **Consciousness**.

> "*The sound vibration, when it is guided by the intention, extends to the entire body that amplifies it like a drum's resonance and produces it like a musical instrument.*"
> — Alfred Tomatis

> "*Working on a symbol awakens all its corresponding forces at all the levels of a being.*" [15]

Among the more familiar **mantras** there is the **AUM** or, in its shortened form, the **Om**. This **mantra** was transmitted to us by

---

15 Mircea Eliade, *Yoga: Immortality and Freedom*, Princeton University Press (2009).

the Himalayan sages. It is the most important **mantra** in Yoga. For Hindus, it is considered to be the primitive divine vibration of the universe that represents all existence. In fact, this **mantra** is located at the summit of the worlds of matter, energy, time, and space on the mental level, where we find the "heaven" of most of the great religions of this world. Further on, we will see that it is rather the **HU mantra** (pronounced Yioo) that plays this role and that I find at the summit of the pure worlds of God beyond the worlds of matter, energy, time, and space. To make a comparison, let us say that if I divide all the worlds of creation into twelve levels, the **AUM mantra** is located at the fifth level and the **HU mantra** is at the twelfth level.

Another very popular **mantra** is: **OM MANI PADME HUM**. According to the Buddhists, **OM MANI PADME HUM** is the **most** mystical **mantra of all**.

OM, the Sun whose Energy adumbrates [16]all things.

MANI, the planetary and human that the Sun's rays must penetrate in order to awaken and expand LIFE.

PADME, a part of eternal knowledge.

HUM, a part of the accomplishment of the Divine in oneself.

I went to India with three people from Quebec. On 5 June 2005 in the north-east of India, at the temple of Kedarnath [17] in the pre-Himalayas, I attended the Maharudrabeshek ceremony,

---

16 Adumbrate: signify, suggest.
17 One of the most sacred sanctuaries dedicated to Shiva, located at one of the three sources of the Ganges, the sacred river of India.

performed for me by 11 priests who, among other things, recited for me the 1,000 names of God, and asked me to chant this mantra, **OM MANI PADME HUM**, continuously throughout the whole two hours the ceremony lasted. It was an elevating experience.

The HU Chant

If I had to remember a single **word** in this book, it would be the **word** "HU," which is pronounced HEOU-OU. If I speak of words that free me, then this **word**, **HU**, is certainly the most significant one in this book.

> *The HU chant is a sound of opening of Conscience, healing, and protection.*

The **HU chant** can be used as an exercise in contemplation. Contemplation consists in **focusing one's attention on something**, whether it is God, the Holy Spirit, or a spiritually elevated being. By this principle, I tend to develop or manifest the qualities of God, the Holy Spirit, or the spiritually elevated being. Contemplation is an active thought process that is very reassuring for us Westerners. With this principle in mind:

> *I become what I choose to put my attention on.*

I just need to sit in a comfortable position, with my back held up straight. I close my eyes and while exhaling chant the **mantra HU** (pronunciation: **HEOU-OU-OU**). I do this for five to twenty minutes a day.

> **HU is a song of Love to God.**

I focus my attention on my third eye, the spot between the eyebrows at the root of the nose, and, while keeping my eyes closed, I visualize an imaginary coin placed there as if I were staring at it without straining, but with a **certain amount of concentration**. Simultaneously, I think of God, the Holy Spirit, or a superior spiritual being.

> **Chanting HU constitutes a chant of Love to God.**

If no conscious experience is felt within 20 minutes, it is best to simply stop. However, experiencing nothing doesn't mean that there isn't anything happening inside me . . . For example, if I spend a sunny day on the beach, even though I don't feel the sun's heat on my skin because of the wind, I'm still being warmed by it. The purpose of this exercise is to raise one's **Consciousness** in a natural and harmonious way in accordance with one's own evolution.

When I engage in a contemplation exercise, I "polarize" my inner bodies toward a spiritual goal. Just as though I were made up of billions of tiny magnets, all magnetically oriented toward a high spiritual goal, all of my bodies become a compass that orients me toward a single goal: Self-Realization, and then to attain God-Realization.

During this exercise, my inner sight perceives different colors or different landscapes. Similarly, my inner ear hears sounds such as the trickling of a stream, the sound of a bagpipes, thousands of violins, booming thunder, tinkling bells, the buzzing of bees, the rustling of wind in the trees, etc. These sights and sounds represent all the elements linked to different planes of creation.

> *The HU chant is a sound that opens the awareness, that heals and protects. The sound HU contains The most elevated vibrations that can be pronounced with the human voice. Attributed to this mantra are virtues related to the protection that I can benefit from if I pronounce it in a situation of danger.*

The Recording of the HU Chant

This **mantra** was recorded in 2003, in the Sélecson Studio in a suburb of Quebec City in Canada, by Productions ATMA Internationales. Several people took part in this recording, some of whom had been practicing this **mantra** for more than 27 years. To give the impression of a crowd, we made the recording several times over several hours, the whole day in fact, in 15-minute periods, and then layered the total recordings together. During the recording, certain participants wore listening devices enabling them to keep the tonality of the universal LA note at 440 cycles per second. The resonance effect gives the impression of an immense cavern in the form of a cathedral that one might find in the Himalayas, or of the echo that the Himalayan Mountain ranges return to us in certain places, as in the Tirmir Valley of Northern Tibet where the **sound** and the **light** come together on certain special occasions. At the moment of the recording, there was the energetic presence of the following Masters: Fubbi Quantz, Gopal Das, Kata Daki, Lai Tsi, Peddar Zask, Rami Nuri, Towart Managi, Wah Z, Yabul Saccabi, Rebazar Tarzs. For all the participants, it was an elevating and enriching experience. Listening to this **mantra** with headphones can enable me to better appreciate all the power and the magnificence of this **mantra**.

You can download The HU Chant at:
https://soundcloud.com/jacques-martel-atma/le-chant-dunivers.

Over the years, various writers have offered insight into the HU Chant. You find more information in the Further Reading section (page 119); here are some excerpts:

From
The Whirling Dervishes: Being an Account of the Sufi Order, known as the Mevlevis and its founder the poet and mystic Mevlana Jalaluddin Rumi, by Shems Friedlander.

> *When the Sheik arrives at his post, he bows, sits on the post, and kisses the floor. All the turners sit, and their cloaks are put on them by those who did not turn in the fourth selam. They have returned to their tombs but in an altered state. The Sheik recites the Fathia, the first sura of the Koran, and all the dervishes kiss the floor and rise. The Sheik then sounds a prayer to Mevlana and Shams Tabriz and begins the sound HU. The dervishes join in sounding the HU which is all the names of God in one.*

From
The Music of Life, by Hazrat Inayat Khan.

> *The mystery of **HU** is revealed to the Sufi who journeys*
> *through the path of initiation. Truth, the knowledge of*
> *God, is called by a Sufi "**haqq**." If we divide the word*
> *haqq into two parts, its assonant sounds become "hu*
> *ek," **HU** signifying God or truth and EK in Hindustani*
> *meaning one. Both together express one God and one*
> *truth. "**Haqiqat**" in Arabic means the essential truth,*
> *"**hakim**." means master, and "**hakim**" means knower, all*
> *of which words express the essential characteristics of life.*
>
> *"**Hur**" in Arabic means the beauties of heavens;*
> *its real meaning is the expression of heavenly beauty.*
> *"**Zahur**" in Arabic means manifestation, especially that*
> *of God in nature. "**Ahura Mazda**" is the name of God*
> *known to the Zoroastrians. The first word, "**Ahura**,"*
> *suggests **HU**, upon which the whole name is built.*
>
> *All of these examples signify the origin of God in the*
> *word **HU** and the life of God in everything and being.*

From
The Religions of Tibet, by Giuseppe Tucci.

> *The figure of the creator, who corresponds to the Isvara*
> *of certain Saivite schools, bear various names, among*
> *them sNang ba ód ldan, Kun snang khyab pa and khri*
> *khug rgyal po. That which he creates has two aspects, the*
> *exterior world ("**phyi snod**") and that contained within it*
> *("**bcud**"), a division that corresponds to that between the*
> *Indian "**bhajana-loka**" and "**sattva-loka**." The cosmology*
> *which is attached to this is surely very old and is throughout*

constructed on a dualist basis. From the breath which
streamed out of the creator there emerged two syllables
HU HU, and progressively, the entire universe.

From
A Dictionary of Egyptian Gods and Goddesses, by George Hart.

HU: The god who personifies the authority of a word of
command.
HU came into being from a drop of blood from the
phallus of the sun god Ré.
When, according to the theology of the Pyramid Age,
the king becomes a lone star, his companion is HU. The
royal authority is maintained in the Afterlife by HU
acknowledging the king's supremacy and allowing the
monarch to cross the waters of his canal.
It is tempting to correlate HU with the power of
the tongue of Ptah in the Memphite creation legend,
commanding the universe into existence, at the instigation of
Ptah's heart ♥.

From
The Secret Teachings of All Ages: An Encyclopedic Outline of
Masonic, Hermetic, Cabbalistic and Rosicrucian Symbolic
Philosophy, by Manly P. Hall.

Godfrey Higgins states that HU, the Mighty, regarded as
the first settler of Britain, came from a place which the
Welsh Triads call the summer country, the present site of
Constantinople. Albert Pike says that the Lost Word of
Masonry is concealed in the name of the Druid god HU.
The meagre information extant concerning the secret

initiations of the Druids indicates a decided similarity between their Mystery school and the schools of Greece and Egypt. HU, the sun God, was murdered and, after several ordeals and mystic rituals, was restored to life.

From
The Flute of God, by Sri Paul Twitchell.

By filling our world with the creative sound of HU, the unknown name of God, we will become a channel for the divine spirit. When used properly, uttered aloud or silently, the creative Soul will enable our Soul to ride the divine vibrations through all the realms of time and space to our own glorious destination.

This spirit, the Voice of HU – HU is often known as the SUGMAD – which is the true name of God in the upper realms, has one great quality and that is to create effect. As it flows down through the worlds, from its fountainhead in the centre of all creation, far above this earth world, it needs distributors, and it works through Souls.

From
Be the HU, by Sri Harold Klemp.

Every moment of your life, you must be the HU. This is more than just chanting HU. This is being the HU. The Sound must always be in your atoms. It must be with you when you're driving, when you're at work, when you're at home eating a meal with your family. The HU and you must be one and the same. And if you make yourself more and more one with the HU, you will find that life is a more joyful place.

PARTICIPANTS' COMMENTS

The HU chant is wonderful to listen to, especially when I'm meditating but also when I want to heighten the vibrations in a room. In meditation, the song helps me find my own centre; it carries me on waves of peace and love. Sometimes, I chant alone but I prefer chanting in a group. It is a powerful self-awareness tool! Thank you!

— *V.R.*

I listen to it mornings and evenings at regular intervals. In the morning, it helps me start my day in calmness far from the stresses of appointments, work, concerns, etc. It extends my period of restfulness and I can tackle the day, being more relaxed and more in tune with my inner being . . . At night, this soft and engaging music helps me to quickly fall asleep and induces a state in which dreams have started happening again.

— *J.D.*

This chant is very effective in helping me re-centre myself. When I start chanting, the first vibrations give me a feeling of evaporation. Then the chant enables me to center myself, rebuild my inner strength and stability. It's very effective.

— *C.L.*

Conclusion

While perusing this book recently, I have become more conscious of the importance of **words** and especially of their power, which can be negative, but mostly positive if I know how to use them properly.

I have often wondered how it could be that some respectable public figures and/or people who have reached a certain level of **Consciousness** use only positive formulations and pay attention to the **words** they use, etc., without anyone having told them to do so.

I have noticed that there comes a time when I can sense the effect of a negative word on me, in the form of distress or discomfort, and that of a positive word, in the form of well-being, comfort, and even freedom. My mind then registers the information to be able, later on, to use only those words or formulations that bring me well-being and comfort.

This book reveals some ways that will enable me to better sense this openness of **Consciousness**, this **freedom** and this **wisdom** that are in me and will give me the opportunity to be able to manifest them more and more.

From 1998 to 2003, I gave workshops in Europe for six to nine months a year almost every weekend. During this period, many people attended my workshops, and some would also later come back as assistants, which enabled them to further integrate what they had previously learned. Their new role as spectators enabled them to gain an overall view of what was taking place in a workshop. Thus, the fact of hearing me often correct participants' formulations led them to modify their choices of words more completely in their own lives.

And several among them later told me, regarding this way of speaking:

> *"You know, Jacques, what I find the most difficult*
> *to experience, now that I've put all these language*
> *issues into practice, it's feeling all the negative*
> *implications emanating from certain **words***
> *that people use and becoming more **aware** of the*
> *limitations they impose on themselves and on others*
> *by using those **words**."*

So, if someone pronounces words that can affect me, the best way I know to counter that is simply to say "**Thanks**" inside of me and, eventually, this drawback will tend to disappear even if the reality remains the same.

After reading this book, I am now more **conscious** of the process of using **words** and the consequences it may have in my life. I am therefore more responsible for improving my lot. However, that requires practice and it's what I do with the people around me, those I work with, in my workshops and lectures. I cannot correct all the people around me, but I must remain open and conciliatory and say "**Thanks**" from the bottom of my **heart ♥** for what I know and what helps me in life.

For my part, I allow myself to correct the people who work with me at my office, because that is part of the group's **Consciousness**, the work environment in which we all evolve, and it gives everyone a better opportunity to work with an openness of **Consciousness**, with more **love**.

I suggest that you practice what you have become more **Conscious** about in this book and you will quickly notice the effects on your **Consciousness** and well-being.

BARAKA BASHAD
May the blessings be!

Further Reading

Allen, James. *As a Man Thinketh*. Independently published, 2022.

Banks, Dr Murray. *Arrêter la terre de tourner, je veux descendre*. Brossard, CA: Un monde différent, 2013.

Banks, Dr Murray. *Au cas où vous croiriez être normal*. Brossard, CA: Un monde différent, 1998.

Banks, Dr Murray. *How to Live with Yourself*. A Murmil Associates Inc., 1965.

Bernier, Lucie and Lenghan, Robert. *The Little Stick Figures Technique for Emotional Self-Healing*. Rochester, VT: Findhorn Press, 2022.

Comment réussir sa vie: Vivre sa vie pour la réussir. Edition Cratere, 2009.

Friedlander, Shems. *The Whirling Dervishes: Being an Account of the Sufi Order, known as the Mevlevis and its founder the poet and mystic Mevlana Jalalúddin Rumi*. New York: State University of New York Press, 1992.

Hall, Manly P. *The Secret Teachings of All Ages: An Encyclopedic Outline of Masonic, Hermetic, Cabbalistic and Rosicrucian Symbolic Philosophy*. Mineola: Dover Publications, 2010.

Hancock, Graham and Bauval, Robert. *The Message of the Sphinx*. New York: Crown, 2009.

Hart, George. *A Dictionary of Egyptian Gods and Goddesses*. Abingdon: Routledge, 1986.

Hill, Napoleon. *The Law of Success*. Wise, VA: The Napoleon Hill Foundation, 2013.

Khan, Hazrat Inayat. *The Music of Life*. Omega Press, 1988.

Klemp, Sri Harold. *Be the HU*. Chanhassen: Eckankar, 1992.

Maltz, Dr Maxwell. *Conquest of Frustration*. New York: Ballantine Books, 1976.

Maltz, Dr Maxwell. *La psycho cybernétique et l'accomplissement de soi*. Brossard, CA: Un monde différent.

Maltz, Dr Maxwell. *Psycho-Cybernetics*. Brossard, CA: Un monde différent, 1983.

Mandino, Og. *The Greatest Secret in the World*. New York: Bantam Books, 1997.

Martel, Jacques. *The Encyclopedia of Ailments and Diseases*. Rochester, VT: Findhorn Press, 2020.

Martel, Jacques. *The 5 Steps to Achieve Healing*. Quebec, CA: Les Éditions ATMA Internationales, 2018.

Packer, Duane and Roman, Sanaya. *Creating Money*, 2nd edition. Novato, CA: H.J. Kramer/New World Library, 2007.

Roussel, Didier. *Fais toi confiance*. 2023.

Scheifele, Jean. *Vivre Dans L'enthousiasme.* Brossard, CA: Un monde différent, 1986.

Schwartz, David J. *La magie de s'auto-diriger.* Brossard, CA: Un monde différent, 2013.

Shinn, George. *The Miracle of Motivation,* revised edition. Carol Stream, IL: Tyndale House Publishers, 1994.

Shuller, Robert. *Plus haut, toujours plus haut.* Brossard, CA: Un monde différent.

Tucci, Giuseppe. *The Religions of Tibet.* Berkeley: University of California Press, 1988.

Twitchell, Sri Paul. *The Flute of God.* London: APG Books, 1969.

Ziglar, Zig. *Rendez-vous au sommet.* Brossard, CA: Un monde différent, 2016.

About the Author

Photo by Serge Bourdages

B orn in Montreal (Canada) in September 1950, Jacques Martel finished his training as an electrical engineer in 1977 at Laval University in Quebec City and became a regular member of the Order of Quebec Engineers. He later taught electricity and electronics for the Canada Manpower Centre (CMC) and also worked as a trainer in private business.

He has always had a keen interest in communication in all its forms. After completing his university studies, electronic media attracted his attention and in 1977 he undertook a training program at the Quebec College of Radio and Television Announcers (CART in French). For the next two years he took part as an anchorman and research assistant in more than 100 episodes of various TV programs on health and well-being that were shown on a private television network throughout the province of Quebec.

His desire to understand the "other side of things" led him on a spiritual quest that completely reoriented his life. In 1978 he undertook research on vitamin therapy, also called the ortho-molecular approach, which follows a holistic path to well-being. His approach dovetailed with that of Canadian, American, and European psychiatrists, researchers, chemists, and biochemists in that field.

In 1988 he undertook personal development training. This training touched such a chord that he became a leader of personal development workshops, an occupation that he then pursued full time as a psychotherapist starting in 1990.

Enriched by the truths he discovered, the communicator in him chose to share the fruits of his reflections with as many people as possible. Thus, the ATMA Growth Centre was born in 1990 and in 1996 it became **ATMA Inc.**, which included **Les Éditions ATMA Internationales** (for books) and **Les Productions ATMA Internationales** (for conferences, guided meditations, and music CDs). Jacques Martel is still the acting president.

Since 1990, he has continued to pursue his personal and professional training, which has enabled him to acquire a solid reputation in this field. It was in 1995 that he acquired his training as a Rebirther (a conscious breathing technique). His vast experience also enables him to act as a consultant with therapists and other health professionals.

In 1991, a writing project emerged in his life. Slowly but surely, the first French edition of the book *The Encyclopedia of Ailments and Diseases* began to take form. The knowledge acquired during his training as an electrical engineer enabled him to learn how to travel from the tangible to the intangible and from practice to intuition; furthermore, his many workshops and conferences confirmed for him the close link between illnesses (ailments and diseases) and thoughts (feelings and emotions) as the sources of conflicts that can lead to the triggering of those illnesses. The book finally appeared in its first edition in April 1998.

He then went on to study the healing energy technique of Reiki, and in 1993 he became a Reiki Master. From 1994 to 1998, he was the President of the Canadian and Quebec Association of Reiki Masters (ACQMR in French). In 2011, he was trained in "Reconnection" (another healing energy technique) and helped others to become reconnected so that they in turn could later be trained to become practitioners of this technique themselves. Since April 2004, he has become more conscious of the Way that must be followed to further develop the means for moving toward physical, emotional, mental, and spiritual healing.

Jacques Martel presents conferences, takes part in health and well-being fairs, and leads workshops internationally. From 1988 to 2013, he led workshops in Europe and in the French D.O.M. (Overseas Territories), on Reunion Island, in French Polynesia, and in Mauritius. He also, upon request, trains other therapists in his emotional healing technique ITHT (*the Integration Through the Heart Technique*) that he has developed in recent years and which has given his clients positive results. He also gives a training session entitled *On the Road to Awakening*, which helps people who wish to open themselves up inside in order to reach further levels of consciousness, safely and sincerely.

He also developed the *Little Stick Figures Technique*, introduced in the book of the same name by Lucie Bernier and Robert Lenghan. It is a powerful and effective technique for becoming more keenly aware of our negative patterns and positively transforming them. Over the years, Jacques Martel has published many books and recordings that originate with his coaching work and are highly appreciated by people seeking healing and well-being.

For more information see: **https://jacquesmartel.com** and **https://atma.ca**.

Also by This Author

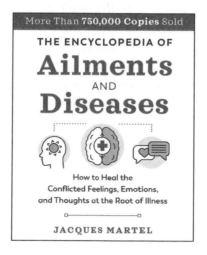

The Encyclopedia of Ailments and Diseases
How to Heal the Conflicted Feelings, Emotions, and Thoughts at the Root of Illness

by Jacques Martel

IN THIS REFERENCE AND HEALING TOOL, Jacques Martel explains how to uncover the conflicted conscious or unconscious feelings, thoughts, and emotions at the root of many illnesses and conditions. He offers healing prompts and affirmations to effect change for nearly 900 different ailments and diseases. Compiling years of research and the results of thousands of cases he encountered in his private practice and during workshops over the past 30 years, Jacques Martel explains how to read and understand the body's language of disease and imbalance.

978-1-64411-189-5

The Little Stick Figures Technique for Emotional Self-Healing

by Lucie Bernier and Robert Lenghan

A PRACTICAL GUIDE to detaching from unhealthy or outdated energetic links with people, emotional patterns, and toxic situations. Developed by Jacques Martel, the Little Stick Figures Technique is an easy energetic cord-cutting method to free yourself from your dependencies, your fears, and your conscious and unconscious attachments. The book explains the 7 simple steps of the technique as well as how to achieve lasting results.

978-1-64411-521-3

FINDHORN PRESS

Life-Changing Books

Learn more about us and our books at
www.findhornpress.com

For information on the Findhorn Foundation:
www.findhorn.org